MORE THAN WINNERS

An Athlete's Study of the Epistles

Elliot Johnson

More Than Winners
©1993 by Full Court Press
P.O. Box 141513
Grand Rapids, Michigan 49514.
All rights reserved

1 2 3 4 5 6 / 97 96 95 94 93
Printed in the United States of America

Cover photo by Victah Sailer

Dedication

*This book is dedicated to
Our Lord and Savior, Jesus Christ,
who has made us
More Than Winners
in the Game of Life!*

Contents

Introduction • 7
The Dynamite of God • 9
God's Unmistakable Record • 11
The Injury Report • 13
Our Need for Adversity • 15
Dying to Win • 17
No Condemnation! • 19
More than Winners • 21
Living Sacrifices • 23
Submission to Authorities • 25
Stepping Stone or Stumbling Block? • 27
The Power of the Weak • 29
Fitness of the Temple • 31
Run to Win • 33
The Escape Route • 35
Gifted by God's Grace • 37
God's Perfect Love • 39
Jesus, the Victor • 41
A Triumphal Procession • 43
Pressed, but not Pinned • 45
The Winner's Circle • 46
An Athletic Ambassador • 48
Same Coach, Same Goals 50
Generous Giving • 52
Man's Power Shortage • 54
Hindrance on the Track • 56
Conflict and the Fruit of Victory • 58
Law of the Harvest • 60
The Victory Platform • 62
Trophies of His Grace • 64
Power on the Inside • 66
Cure for Callousness • 68
The Power of Words • 70
God's Uniform • 72
Winners Either Way • 74
Humility and Honor • 76
A Single Goal • 78

Contents (Continued)

Mind of a Winner • 80
The Real "Number One" • 82
Revelation of a Mystery • 85
Victory after the Conflict • 87
The Internal Umpire • 89
Takeover by Heart and Spirit • 91
Smelling the Finish Line • 93
Attitude Check • 95
Never too Young to Win • 97
Flee, Follow, and Fight • 99
Overcoming Fear by Faith • 101
Competing by the Rules • 103
Right Information about God • 105
Run to Finish • 107
Once for All-Time • 109
Isolated at the Goal Line • 111
The Hall of Faith • 113
Eyes on the Goal • 115
The Discipline of Training • 117
Contentment and a No-Cut Contract • 119
The Marathon of Life • 121
Murder with a Small, Deadly Weapon • 123
Man's Plans and God's Sovereignty • 125
Destined to Win • 127
The Pressure and the Purpose • 129
Lion on a Chain • 131
Get Up and Breathe! • 133
The Love God Hates • 135
We Grow Because We Know • 137
Deceived by an Imposter • 139
Glory! • 141
Poor Representatives • 143
The Tragedy of Delay • 145
A New Beginning • 147

Introduction

FOR THOUSANDS OF YEARS, athletic competition between opposing teams has provided recreation and diversion for spectators. These struggles captivated audiences during the early days of the apostle Paul and others who penned the New Testament letters. Often, it is necessary to understand the athletic events of the day if we intend to understand the Scriptures! With this in mind, let us review the history of athletics, especially the history of the Greek Olympic games and the contests that took place during the rise of the Roman Empire.

The Greek ideal of a sound mind in a sound body was personified by their athletic competitions, especially in the sport of gymnastics. Youthful Greeks began at age seven and worked out every day during their careers. The ancient Olympics began around 850 B.C., though no records of these games were kept until 776 B.C. Every four years, in honor of the god Zeus, the Greeks ceased all wars and engaged in athletic competition. The province of Olympia was sacred, with its plantations, great buildings and thousands of statues. This one province had permanent freedom tests, the Isthmian Games (honoring the god Poseidon), the Pythian Games (honoring Apollo) and the Nemea Games (honoring Zeus) were also held. As Greek influence faded and Christianity increased, the games were banned (393 A.D.) and faded from existence until 1896 when Pierre deCoubertin of France developed the modern Olympics.

As Roman civilization and power advanced, the emperors constructed at least 270 great amphitheaters throughout the empire. The Colosseum in Rome seated 50,000 and the one in Scarus seated 80,000. The stadium at Ephesus, where Paul stayed for three years, was frequently the site of the Olympics. It seated 100,000 spectators. The Circus Maximus, used for boxing, racing, and wrestling in the 4th century, reportedly seated 385,000 people! It was large enough to flood the arena and stage mock sea battles. In time the focus of the events shifted from sports contests to violent combat. As the empire degenerated and fans thirsted for more and more violence, contests between man and wild beast became routine. As social outcasts of the day, Christians were butchered in honor of the pagan Roman gods. Thousands died in these arenas to satiate the bloody lusts of the Romans.

Into this society came the good news of salvation by faith in the shed blood of the Lord Jesus Christ. Paul and other writers traveled throughout the empire relating the gospel in the language of athletic competition. "Enter into conflict," "fight the good fight," "run the race," the "rewards platform," and "victory" were used to explain the Christian life. Beyond any other theme, the great message of the apostles to the early churches was that despite fierce opposition in the game of life, followers of Jesus Christ are *More Than Winners* (Romans 8:37)! Because of His mighty power at work within us, we can do all things through Christ (Philippians 4:13). And best of all, we will one day be just like our Master (Romans 8:29)!

The message to believers today is the same as it was to first century Christians: We are *More Than Winners!* As you study the letters of the New Testament may your commitment to the Christ who has given you eternal victory grow ever stronger.

Read Romans 1:1-17

THE DYNAMITE OF GOD

I am not ashamed of the gospel, because it is the power of God for the salvation of everyone who believes: first for the Jew, then for the Gentiles.

Romans 1:16

HIS STUDENTS LAUGHED at him when Los Angeles high school math teacher Mike Larrabee began working out for the 1964 Tokyo Olympics. Unashamedly, Larrabee continued training for the 400 meters. At the age of 30, he beat the odds and became the first white person in 32 years to win the 400-meter race!. Now everyone knew he had no need to be ashamed of his efforts or their results!

Likewise, when a man is a winner in Christ, he has no reason to be ashamed when others criticize him for his stand. The Apostle Paul expressed this bold confidence in Romans 1:16 when he said that he was unashamed of the gospel of Christ because "it is the power of God for the salvation of *everyone* who believes!" He used the Greek word "dunamis" (from which we get our word "dynamite") to describe the mighty power of God to save sinners by raising Jesus from the dead! Paul goes on to explain that the Jews, as chosen by Him to be the "custodians" of the gospel (3:2) and the people through whom the Messiah came (9:5), first received the message. Then, it was made clear to non-Jews.

When a man is saved by the "dynamite" of God, the righteousness of Christ is imputed ("reckoned to his account") to justify the man on the basis of faith! This gospel is "Good News" - not good advice on how to live. It tells us not what we must do to earn salvation, but what Christ has done! The gospel is not a philosophy of life or a code of ethics, but a person - Jesus Christ! We are saved by faith and we live and die by faith (v.17)!

Have you ever been made light of — verbally or otherwise — because of your faith in the gospel of Christ? If so, you're in good company! All winners in Christ suffer to some degree. Accept the scorn of the world, but never be ashamed of the dynamic power of God which saved you! One day, the Lord Jesus will reveal the real winners!

QUESTIONS:

1. How does the world system put Christians down?
2. How can unbelieving friends subtly insult believers?
3. How does the gospel differ from a code of ethics?

ACTION POINT:

Stand unashamedly for the gospel of Christ.

Read Romans 1:18-32

GOD'S UNMISTAKABLE RECORD

For since the creation of the world, God's invisible qualities - His eternal power and divine nature — have been clearly seen, being understood from what has been made, so that men are without excuse.

Romans 1:20

THE RECORD BOOKS SAY that John Anderson won the discus event in the 1932 Olympics. But Jules Noël of France was the real news-maker, for on his fourth throw he launched a throw that appeared to land beyond Anderson's first place effort. Unfortunately, every official was distracted at the time by the tense competition in the nearby pole vault. No one saw where Noël's throw landed! Embarrassed, the officials awarded the Frenchman an extra throw, but he came nowhere close and had to return home without a medal!

The judges of the discus in the 1932 Olympics resemble the rest of mankind in considering the record of God's revelation to man. Romans 1 tells us that our gracious God has plainly revealed truth to all men (v. 19). Creation itself reveals His nature and His Power (Ps. 19:1-4, 97:6). Yet, men turn their backs to God and, in their wickedness, suppress the truth (v. 18). In His "Supreme Court," the God of Heaven "gives men over" to progressively lower and lower forms of degradation: worship of created things (v. 25), homosexuality (v. 26-27) and other forms of wickedness (v. 29-31). Clearly, apart from God, man never evolves upward, but he degenerates to a level lower than animals. No animal is ever homosexual or kills its unborn young. Further darkness, ignorance and specific mental and physical diseases (v. 27) are the due penalty for perversion. Yet, our God's record of Himself is clear to see:

The heavens declare the glory of God;
the skies proclaim the work of His hands.
Day after day they pour forth speech;
night after night they display knowledge.
There is no speech or language
where their voice is not heard.
Their voice goes out into all the earth,
their words to the ends of the world.

Psalm 19:1-4

God is not sitting idly by trying to keep people out of heaven. When any man responds to the light given, God gives more light so that he may be saved! Our loving and just God rejoices when men respond to that light!

QUESTIONS:

1. Why is God just in separating Himself from those who reject Him?
2. What are some natural consequences of sin?
3. How does God send more light when men respond to given light?

ACTION POINT:

Respond to the light God gives you.

Read Romans 3:1-26

THE INJURY REPORT

. . . for all have sinned and fall short of the glory of God and are justified freely by His grace through the redemption that came by Christ Jesus.

Romans 3:23-24

SILVIO LEONARD certainly spent enough time in the training room during his career. The winner of the 100-meter run in the 1975 Pan American Games in Mexico City pulled a muscle as he crossed the finish line and fell into the 10-foot moat that surrounded the track! Though seriously injured, he recovered to qualify for the 1976 Olympics in Montreal. However, ten days prior to the races he cut his foot during a bit of horseplay and was eliminated in the quarterfinals. The injury report on Silvio could read "accident prone" and "eliminated from competition."

God has called the whole world into His "training room" for a spiritual examination. He gives us the Law so that we might look into it as a mirror and see ourselves (v. 20). His diagnosis: no one is righteous (v. 10); all of us are spiritually "accident prone." All have sinned (v. 23) and fallen short of God's glory (the "outward manifestation of God's attributes"). Mankind's "severe injury" must be understood. God calls it "sin" (used over 60 times in the book of Romans). It is an archery term meaning "to miss the mark." It is defined as lawlessness (1 Jn. 3:4). All of us are sinners by being related to the first sinner, Adam (Rom. 5:12). All of us are sinners by choice. Indeed, we act as we do because of what we are!

What is God's prognosis of man's future in sin? Romans 6:23 says that the wages of sin is death (eternal separation from God). All are unfit to participate in the game of life. We have no hope of ever getting "back into the game" by our own ingenuity, or in our own power.

Does God have a remedy for this fatal disease? *YES!* He took the initiative to seek us out! Though verse 11 says that no man seeks after God, God sought after man! God may be "found" by receiving justification in Christ Jesus! What does it mean to be justified? Justification is a legal term

13

meaning "to be declared (not made) righteous". It's "Just-as-if-I'd" never sinned to God. *How can a just God justly justify unjust sinners?* Because a sinless Christ took the penalty in His own body on Calvary's cross! God redeemed us ("bought us back") from the curse of our own sin! Can we do anything to merit this healing? *NO!* Because if we could, it would destroy the principle of salvation by grace alone! The healing is totally the work of The Great Physician!

What about you? Have you seen the "Team Doctor" about the sin which keeps you out of the game of life? He has the perfect remedy: the blood of His wonderful Son. You will be saved forever only by receiving His remedy.

QUESTIONS:
1. What is sin?
2. Who prescribes the only cure for sin?
3. Why can we do nothing to earn salvation?

ACTION POINT:

Praise God for His remedy for your sin.

Read Romans 5:1-11

OUR NEED FOR ADVERSITY

. . . but we also rejoice in our sufferings, because we know that suffering produces perseverance; perseverance, character; and character, hope. And hope does not disappoint us, because God has poured out His love into our hearts by the Holy Spirit, whom He has given us.

Romans 5:3-5

HUNGARIAN MARKSMAN Karoly Varga broke his shooting hand two days before the 1980 Olympics Small-bore Rifle Competition and had to compete with a bandaged hand. An injury of this type would have been discouraging to most people, but Varga (who won the Gold medal) explained that the injury actually helped him, because it forced him to squeeze the trigger more delicately. Maybe more marksmen should welcome the adversity that Varga experienced!

Just as adversity was an asset to Karoly Varga, suffering is indispensable (and inevitable) in the lives of Christians! Those whom God has justified by faith (v.1) have a reason (and a power) to rejoice in adverse circumstances.

When suffering comes, what is the right response? We are to "welcome trials as friends" (James 1:2-4). In a society where endurance is becoming increasingly rare (if people don't like their mates, they go get a divorce), character is out of style (if people don't like the law, they go around it), and hope is fading (most people are pessimistic about the future), the Christian who rejoices in adversity develops all these character traits! In fact, it is only through adversity and joyful acceptance of suffering that Christlikeness is developed!

This response is totally foreign to the natural response of the world. To the unbeliever, joy is only possible when things are going as he desires. But the believer in Christ has power from God to rejoice in trials. We know that if God loved and saved us while we were still sinners (5:8), how much more is our future secured from His wrath (v. 9). The present ministry of intercession by the living Christ keeps us saved (Heb. 7:25) and guarantees our future!

Christian, next time you suffer, praise and thank God! He has sent invaluable difficulty to refine and bring out the best — the character of Christ — within you. You'd never become like Jesus without it.

QUESTIONS:
1. Why is adversity essential?
2. What is the proper response to adversity?
3. Who has a reason to rejoice in suffering?

ACTION POINT:

Thank God for every adversity in your life.

Read Romans 6:1-14

DYING TO WIN

For we know that our old self was crucified with him so that the body of sin might be rendered powerless, that we should no longer be slaves to sin.

Romans 6:6

SOON AFTER THE APOSTLE PAUL wrote the book of Romans, the Emperor Nero amused himself with bloody gladiatorial combat and with the torture of Christians. A parade of gladiators (Lat. gladius; sword) in full armour opened ceremonies in the great Coliseum. They presented their weapons and cried "Hail O Caesar; those about to die greet thee!" The ensuing bloodshed satiated the sick Roman culture. For two centuries, millions of Christians were slain under various rulers. Christians were killed for their refusal to worship the Emperor (under Trajan) or for refusing to sacrifice to the pagan gods in general (under Decius). Think of it! By simply taking a pinch of incense and throwing it on an altar, men, women and children could save themselves from such suffering. But the Lordship of Christ in their lives refused to allow them to do so! In 1927 a simple cross was erected in the Coliseum in honor of the martyrs before the ruins of the royal box. Inscribed at its base were the words "Hail to Thee, O Cross, the Only Hope!" Christianity had spread around the world. Certainly Tertullian was right when he wrote at the end of the 2nd century, "The blood of the martyrs is the seed of the church."

Just as martyrs have "died to win" throughout history, individual believers must count themselves dead to sin so that the power of Christ may win in them. Romans 6:6 tells us that we were crucified with Christ when He died on the cross. Our old nature is "rendered powerless" (not "eradicated" or "annihilated") *positionally* by His death, so that by counting ourselves dead in *experience* (v. 11) and offering ourselves to God (v. 13) the power of Christ may work through us. Galatians 2:20 says, "I have been crucified with Christ and I no longer live, but Christ lives in me!"

This is Christian living - not the Christian trying to be good, but the Christian counting on Christ to live through him.

We experience a great civil war in this life. Satan, old habits, and the pull of the world all work through that old nature to try to trip us up (Gal. 5:17). Paul wrote of the inner battle he fought daily (7:21-25). He (and we) can only live above sin by constant faith in Christ and His ability to live His life in us. Prayer, meditating on the Word and sensitivity to the Spirit of God are vital. But it can be done!

Next time you feel tempted or even "lukewarm" inside, die to your own desires and feed your mind on Christ. He will win every battle. All you must do to win is die!

QUESTIONS:
1. What is Christian living?
2. How can your experience in Christ better match your position in Christ?
3. Why is a Christian who lives selfishly so miserable?

ACTION POINT:

Thank God that through Christ you can live above sin and self!

Read Romans 8:1-17

NO CONDEMNATION!

Therefore, there is now no condemnation for those who are in Christ Jesus, Because through Christ Jesus the law of the Spirit of life set me free from the law of sin and death.
Romans 8:1-2

THE FUTURE LOOKED BLEAK for Viktor Chukarin when he was thrown into a concentration camp during World War II. The young Ukrainian suffered the condemnation of four years of ill treatment at the hands of his captors. But after the war he was freed, and in the 1952 Olympics Viktor won six medals in gymnastics at Helsinki! Four years later, Viktor (now a 35 year-old teacher) earned five more medals at Melbourne for a remarkable total of eleven medals, including seven golds! A once-condemned prisoner had become an Olympic champion.

Just as Chukarin was freed from the condemnation of prison camp, believers are freed forever from the condemnation of eternal hell! Romans 8 says that those who are "in Christ" are assured that the Spirit (used 19 times in the chapter) frees them from the law of sin and death. In spite of Paul's failures in chapter 7, he knew he never could lose his salvation. Instead of being controlled by the sinful nature, the Apostle was regularly empowered to live by the Spirit of God!

All Christians have the indwelling power of God's Holy Spirit (v. 9) and therefore have the freedom and power to do right. Positionally, we are co-heirs with Christ of all the glories of Heaven (v. 17). Experientially, however, we will suffer while in this world. Our need is not more dedication of self-effort, for Jesus said that apart from Him we could do nothing (John 15:5). Our need is to simply believe that a powerful God can and will work through us to glorify Himself (in pleasure or in pain) and to enjoy the wonderful freedom that He gives!

19

QUESTIONS:

1. Why is there no condemnation for believers?
2. What is the lifestyle of all true believers?
3. What do believers share with Christ?

ACTION POINT:

Let the Spirit of God control you continually.

Read Romans 8:18-39

MORE THAN WINNERS

And we know that in all things God works for the good of those who love Him, who have been called according to His purpose.
Romans 8:28

For those God foreknew He also predestined to be conformed to the likeness of His Son . . .
Romans 8:29

. . . If God is for us, who can be against us?
Romans 8:31

. . . in all these things we are more then conquerors through him who loved us.
Romans 8:37

IT WAS AN OVERMATCHED USA hockey squad that faced the mighty Russians in the 1980 Winter Olympic series. College players from across America took on seasoned veterans trained in the USSR. Coach Herb Brooks frankly told his players, "Gentlemen, you don't have enough talent to win on talent alone." With his words ringing in their ears, the American team pulled off the greatest upset in hockey and possibly in all of Olympic history. Each individual clearly needed something beyond himself to overcome a giant adversary. Yet, without a powerful Russian team opposing them, they could never have risen to such heights! The adversity was needed to transform the Americans into all they could become on the ice!

Though we hesitate to admit it, believers in Jesus need the obstacles that He brings into our lives. God knows what set of circumstances will be effective in conforming each of His children to the likeness of Christ as He has predestined! We, the *justified,* will eventually be just like Jesus (v. 28) and will be *glorified* with Him (v. 30)! He has promised to finish the work He began in us (Phil. 1:6).

What has happened in your life that you never would have wanted to occur? Have you made a serious "mistake," been involved in some "accident," or were you victimized in some way? If not now, later on, you will look back and say, "It was the best thing that could have happened in my life." It left deep impressions that were never forgotten, taught valuable lessons about life, or made you totally dependent upon God. You would never desire to go through such adversity again and would flee from such circumstances, but now that it has happened you thank God that in His sovereignty He allowed it for your good! God met you in your deepest crisis and He proved to be all you needed.

As J. Vernon McGee says, "We entered this chapter with no condemnation; we conclude it with no separation; and in between all things work together for your good!" Truly, we are More Than Winners because the victory is His on our behalf! We don't need to struggle and strain to achieve what Christ has already achieved! Someday our faith will become sight and we'll understand all the reasons behind what has happened. That will be a great day. Until then, if God is for us, who can be against us?

QUESTIONS:
1. Who will we be like someday?
2. How does God get us there?
3. What can separate us from God's love?

ACTION POINT:

Live like the winner God has made you.

Read Romans 12:1-21

LIVING SACRIFICES

Therefore, I urge you, brothers, in view of God's mercy, to offer your bodies as living sacrifices, holy and pleasing to God — this is your spiritual worship. Do not conform any longer to the pattern of this world, but be transformed by the renewing of your mind. Then you will be able to test and approve what God's will is — His good, pleasing and perfect will.

Romans 12:1-2

BORN IN TIENTSIN, CHINA, to Scottish missionary parents in 1902, Eric Liddell grew up loving the Lord. After age five he moved to Scotland where he gained a tremendous reputation as an inspired trackman. The "Flying Scot", upon whose life the film "Chariots of Fire" is based, qualified in the 100-meters in the 1924 Olympics, but withdrew because of his conviction not to run on a Sunday. Instead, he spent part of the day giving a sermon in a church in Paris. Later in the same Olympics, Eric qualified and *won* the 400-meters in a spectacular time of 47.6 seconds! He became a national hero in Scotland. A year later Eric returned to China to join his father in missionary work. He was there during World War II and died of a brain tumor in a Japanese prison camp on February 21, 1945.

Just as Eric Liddell gave his entire life to glorify God, Paul urges all believers to do the same. In chapter 12 Paul outlines the practical application of the great doctrines taught in the early chapters of Romans. He urges Christians to "offer your bodies as living sacrifices" to the Lord. Notice, he urges (not commands) us, for Paul knows we are not under the law but under grace. God desires our sincere heart-felt devotion to himself. He wants our entire physical body, which is our only means of expression and therefore our only means of bringing glory to Him. We are to be *"living* sacrifices!" It is possible to die for Him, but He wants us to live for Him! This is not to earn or to keep our salvation, but to know His will for us and to *glorify* Him! This is our spiritual worship (KJV: "reasonable service") to Him.

23

In presenting ourselves to God we are not to be conformed ("pressed into a mold") to the godless pattern of this world. Instead of floating along the course of least resistance, we are to stand for God against the tide of this evil age. The Holy Spirit will transform us, forming the image of Christ in us! Practically, this means we won't have an exaggerated opinion of our own importance (v. 3) and we will use our spiritual gifts to build up other Christians (v. 4-8). We will keep that "spiritual fervor" in serving Christ (v. 11). We will love others sincerely (v. 9-10). We will be joyful, patient, prayerful, sharing, forgiving, sympathetic, humble, and peaceful people (v. 12-20). While under the control of God's Spirit, we will not be overcome by the flood tide of evil in today's wicked world (v.21). Instead, like Eric Liddell, we will walk straight through this world as victors with our eyes only upon Jesus!

QUESTIONS:
1. What does it mean to be a "living sacrifice?"
2. How are we "transformed?"
3. How is your life different now that you have become a Christian?

ACTION POINT:

Offer your body totally to God.

Read Romans 13:1-7

SUBMISSION TO AUTHORITIES

Everyone must submit himself to the governing authorities, for there is no authority except that which God has established.

Romans 13:1

JIM THORPE became a national hero in 1912 when he won the decathlon in Stockholm, Sweden. But in January of 1913, it was revealed that he had received $25 a week for playing minor league baseball in North Carolina. In the most strict definition of the word, Thorpe was not an amateur. The AAU struck his name from its record books and the United States Olympic Committee apologized to the International Olympic Committee, which revoked Thorpe's medals and trophies. Much later in history (1943) a movement to reinstate Jim's records and trophies was initiated, and finally in 1983 the ban against him was lifted and his gold medals were presented to his children.

Whether Jim Thorpe was ignorant of the rules governing amateurism or not, he was technically guilty in the eyes of the law. The governing authority (U.S.O.C.) had the authority to revoke his medals. The Bible says that God has established all governing authorities (*both* good ones and bad ones) for the purpose of controlling chaos in civilization. Because of the sinful nature of man, without government we would have terrible confusion. The purpose therefore, of government is to protect citizens who do right and to punish lawbreakers (v. 4). Unless a law conflicts with the direct command of God, we are to submit to our governing authorities. Civil government is even given the right of capital punishment for certain offenses (Rom. 13:4)! We are to submit to those over us not only because of possible punishment, but also because our own conscience should tell us to submit (v. 5).

Submission to authorities includes parents, employers, teachers, coaches, referees, and law enforcement officers. Christians must give due respect to all of these authorities as well as to Christian leaders (Heb. 13:17). Practically, this

25

means we are to work heartily for the bosses who pay us, obey parents as long as we are living under their roof, respect teachers and officials and fulfill the commands of our coaches. It means obeying traffic laws and paying taxes. God even commands us to pray for those over us (1 Tim. 2:1-3)!

It was unfortunate that Jim Thorpe lost his medals, but it would be more unfortunate to have no governing body to enforce rules. Next time you become frustrated with an authority, thank God for His appointed messengers who are there to protect and guide you and the rest of society.

QUESTIONS:
1. What would life be like without government?
2. What should your attitude be towards authority?
3. Can you state two reasons for obeying authorities?

ACTION POINT:

Thank God for authorities in your life.

Read Romans 14:1-23

STEPPING STONE OR STUMBLING BLOCK?

Therefore let us stop passing judgment on one another. Instead, make up your mind not to put any stumbling block or obstacle in your brother's way.

Romans 14:13

WHILE THE RULES of soccer permit intercepting the ball from the opponent, they certainly do not allow tripping, holding, or pushing one's opponent. Such play is not only contrary to the rules, but it has also caused international incidents, for soccer fans tend to become very emotional about their national soccer teams. For example, on May 24, 1964, in a pre-Olympic qualifying match in Lima, Peru, 328 people were killed and over 500 injured in one soccer riot. The riot took place after a goal was nullified because of rough play!

God's principles of Christian living don't allow us to put any unintentional hindrance (stumbling block) or intentional trap (obstacle) in our brother's way either (v. 13). How can this happen? Let's look at a few facts pointed out in Romans 14.

First, there are sincere differences of opinion on certain practices about which the Bible is silent. (These issues do not include adultery, theft, and drunkenness, for on these Scripture is clear). In Paul's day, the debate was over eating meat which had possibly been offered to idols and concerning which day to go to church. Today, Christians differ on such things as going to movies and playing card games. Paul tells us that those who have a conscience which enables them to do these things (strong) ought not to judge those whose conscience won't allow these things (weak). Likewise the weak are not to judge the strong on these matters. If there is any doubt in our minds about an action, we should refrain (v. 23). We must act from faith without making our personal conviction an issue (v. 22-23). We must never force our convictions upon others, for each believer is accountable to God (v. 12). Nevertheless, if an action we are free to do would cause our Christian friend to

27

stumble or fall into a trap, we should refrain from that action on the basis of our love for him. Our entire motive must be to build others up (v.19).

Do your convictions differ from others? In some way, they probably do. Don't cause a "riot" in your relationships by these minute differences. Let your life be a stepping stone to build others rather than a stumbling block to hinder them!

QUESTIONS:
1. What other issues divide Christians today?
2. How do you feel about these issues?
3. How can you show love to those who disagree?

ACTION POINT:

Do everything by faith and in love toward others.

Read 1 Corinthians 1:18-31

THE POWER OF THE WEAK

But God chose the foolish things of the world to shame the wise; God chose the weak things of the world to shame the strong.

1 Corinthians 1:27

COACHES did not consider Mack Robinson of Pasadena, California, to be very promising athletic material as a young man. In fact, they made his mother sign a statement absolving them of blame if his heart was damaged during training. Yet Mack did not throw in the towel. He got local businessmen to pay his way to the Olympic trials and he made the team. In 1936, at the Berlin games he ran a 21.1 in the 200 meters and finished second to the great Jesse Owens' record time of 20.7. Mack brought home the silver medal and until his younger brother, Jackie, broke into the major leagues, he was the best known athlete of the Robinson family.

Many religious experts view the gospel of the cross as insignificant today. They look with disdain at God's children who actively teach that man must be born again in order to see the kingdom of God (John 3:3). The preaching of salvation by grace through the shed blood of Christ is foolishness to those who think they can earn God's favor (v.18). The world says that we need better education to cure the ills of man. The world tries to solve society's external problems with legislation and programs. But mankind really needs the gospel of Christ to heal an internal disease — the cancer of sin. The gospel is God's remedy for sin and its effects. The blood of Christ does a thorough job of curing our ills. It is the only remedy that works!

Those who preach the gospel are considered foolish by the world's standards. The carriers of the gospel are usually not the movie stars, industrial tycoons, or governmental officials. God seems to major in average people as examples of His grace (v.26). They preach a simple message that is despised by the world.

Why does God turn the world's standards upside down and use the common man? He does it so that no one may boast in

29

himself (v.29). God's power shows up best in weak people. We are what we are because He is who He is! No academic degree, monetary wealth or position of power is a reason for boasting. He can only boast of the glory and grace of God in Christ Jesus. In our own resources we are nothing. God in His power is everything!

QUESTIONS:
1. How do lost people view the message of the cross?
2. Why does God choose weak people to speak His word?
3. What is man's only cause for boasting?

ACTION POINT:

Thank God that your weaknesses best reveal His strength.

Read 1 Corinthians 6:12-20

FITNESS OF THE TEMPLE

Do you not know that your body is a temple of the Holy Spirit, who is in you, whom you have received from God? You are not your own; you were bought at a price. Therefore honor God with our body.

1 Corinthians 6:19-20

Partly because of their emphasis upon war, the ancient Greeks placed a premium on physical fitness. In fact, it was their interest in fitness which contributed greatly to the idea of the Olympic games. Their motto was "a healthy mind in a healthy body," and the physical education of young people was important from childhood through adulthood.

Long before the Greeks, God designed man's body and provided an ideal environment for his health. In our age, when a person accepts Christ as Savior, God's Spirit actually comes to dwell within the body. This fact gives great importance to the physical body of a Christian. Throughout the Old Testament the glory of God dwelt in a magnificent temple for which He gave specific instructions concerning layout and design. The temple which Solomon built was one of the seven wonders of the ancient world.

Today God does not dwell in a temple made with human hands. Rather, He dwells in the human bodies of believers who trust Him for salvation. Therefore, Paul tells the Corinthian Christians of the importance of caring for their bodies — God's temple. While there was liberty in eating meat, they must not indulge in sexual sin. All sex outside of marriage is sin. This was hard for the loose-living Corinthians to understand. Temple prostitution had long been a part of the heathen religion that they practiced before becoming Christians. Yet, it was a serious matter, for sex is a union which alters the personality of both partners — for good or evil. Christians are one in spirit with God and sexual sin robs God of control of the body that belongs to Him.

Other personal habits are also important for a Christian, for the body where God dwells must reflect His glory. This implies personal cleanliness, wise dietary habits, optimal amounts of sleep, and regular exercise. In fact, if we study the mechanics of body function, we realize it was designed for exercise. Psychologists tell us that three forty-five minute exercise sessions per week are the minimum we need to maintain fitness.

Salvation is free but it is not cheap. Your salvation cost Christ a terribly high price (1 Pet. 1:18-19). He gave Himself —His happiness, His comfort, His glory, His body — to redeem you. Because He bought you, He *owns* you. He is the Buyer, the Price, and the Owner of your body! He will take the responsibility to food, clothe and direct you (Matt. 6:25-33). You have no right to harm your body by gluttony, sexual misconduct, drunkenness, or inactivity. You are to be a better steward of His property than you were before you knew Christ and His purchasing power.

QUESTIONS:
1. Who owns the body that you occupy?
2. How can you honor God with your body?
3. How do men dishonor God with their bodies?

ACTION POINT:

Honor God with your body.

Read 1 Corinthians 9:24-27

RUN TO WIN

Do you not know that in a race all the runners run, but only one gets the prize? Run in such a way as to get the prize.
1 Corinthians 9:24

EDWIN MOSES was named *Sports Illustrated's* 1984 Sportsman of the Year for good reason. Beginning in 1977 and entering the 1984 Olympics, this 400M hurdles champion won 89 consecutive finals races, not to mention all his preliminary heats! His second gold medal of the Olympics became the crowning achievement of this unprecedented winning streak.

Like all other competitors, Edwin Moses ran to win. But during his streak, Edwin was the only competitor to succeed! The Apostle Paul writes to Christians about running a more important race — the great race of faith — with similar determination to win! In this race, all believers can win! Paul's examples of events in the Isthmian Games (held on alternate years near Corinth) were clear to the Corinthians. He knew the winner received only a pine wreath to wear around his head until it withered (v.25). But Christians are to pursue life with a view to the eternal rewards God will one day bestow in Heaven!

Earning these rewards requires personal discipline. Discipline of our minds, our use of time, as well as of our eating and exercise habits are included. Saying "no" to temptation and to worldly pursuits and pleasures is also noted by God. It may mean sacrifice of the *good* for the *best* in serving our Lord. We must *run* in a straight line against the values of the world, *wrestle* intensely against evil forces of darkness (Eph. 6:10-18), and *box* purposely against our own sinful nature (v.26-27). Paul uses a boxing term ("beat my body") from the ancient matches. With hands bound in ox-hides, the contestants attempted to deliver a decisive blow beneath the eye of their opponents for a TKO. Paul says we must deal such a blow to *our own bodies,* rendering them unresponsive to our sinful natures! His fear was that after preaching (Gk. "keryxas" — to summon others to the race), he himself would be disqualified (v.27) and would lose his own reward. Though Paul (and all Christians) could never lose his *salvation* (a free gift of God by grace), he could lose the *rewards* he might earn from God in Heaven for faithfulness on earth!

How are you "running the race" of faith? Don't become lazy and be "benched" by God, losing out on the eternal rewards you could win! Instead, "get in the race" for His glory and for your good!

QUESTIONS:
1. Who runs in the race of faith?
2. Why are we running?
3. How can rewards be earned?

ACTION POINT:

Run the race of faith to WIN!

Read 1 Corinthians 10:1-13

THE ESCAPE ROUTE

No temptation has seized you except what is common to man. And God is faithful; He will not let you be tempted beyond what you can bear. But when you are tempted, He will also provide a way out so that you can stand up under it.

1 Corinthians 10:13

THE MODERN PENTATHLON — made up of horseback riding, fencing, pistol shooting, swimming, and running — may have been derived from an ancient legend. A musketeer of the king escaped from an enemy dungeon and stole a horse. When his horse was shot, he stole a sword and killed a pursuer. With the dead man's pistol, he shot his way through enemy territory to a river. He swam the river and ran the rest of the way to safety! The multiple obstacles facing the musketeer are duplicated in the Olympic pentathlon.

Just as the musketeer faced numerous obstacles in his flight to freedom, the Christian faces numerous temptations as he endeavors to live for Jesus Christ in today's society. Yet, in all these temptations, God has encouraging words for us.

First, we must not think we're the only one being tempted. Every believer faces the same types of temptation (v.13). It's part of being a Christian and a human being!

Second, God is faithful to His children. He never leaves us or forsakes us (Heb. 13:5).

Third, God never allows us to be tempted beyond our capacity to endure by His power. He knows our strengths and weaknesses, our maturity and our childishness. Because He sovereignly controls circumstances, He wisely keeps some trials away from our path while allowing others to come into our lives. Some of God's choicest servants have withstood great trials through strength of character which God has developed in them.

Finally, God sends a way of escape right along with each temptation that comes into our lives. All we have to do is look for the escape route and use it to flee the temptation. We

35

have no excuse to sin, because God's way out is always there! Though we may suffer, we need not sin against our God!

Like the musketeer, are you facing multiple obstacles in the form of temptations? Don't despair, for all Christians face similar trials. Look for the way out that God provides to enable you to live above sin. By taking God's escape route, you can bear up under anything!

QUESTIONS:
1. What is your greatest temptation?
2. What means of escape has God given you?
3. How many others do you know who are similarly tempted?

ACTION POINT:

Look for the way to avoid sin when tempted.

Read 1 Corinthians 12:1-31

GIFTED BY GOD'S GRACE

There are different kinds of gifts, but the same Spirit.
1 Corinthians 12:4

JAPAN'S HIDEO IIJIMA reached the Olympic semifinals of the men's 100 meters in both 1964 and 1968. Considered the fastest sprinter in Japanese history, he attracted the attention of scouts for the Lotte Orions baseball team, who signed him as a pinch-runner and base-stealer. His legs were insured for 50 million yen! However, Iijima hadn't played baseball since he was 12 years-old, and had no knack for getting a jump on the pitcher or sliding. After two years, during which he stole only 23 out of 40 bases, he was released by the team. His physical gift was evidently more related to track than to baseball.

The moment a person receives Christ as his personal Savior, he is given one or more spiritual gifts by our Heavenly Father. God does not haphazardly gift us (v.11), but He assigns gifts according to His perfect will (v.18)! It is important for us to discover and to use the gifts we were given for His glory. We are not all gifted alike and should not be jealous of someone else's gift. Some can sing a song, others can teach a Bible class. Some can administer a project, others can greatly encourage people who are suffering. We are not responsible for gifts we don't possess, but only for those we do possess. All are to be used for the glory of God and the good of others.

It is important to find the type of job where your gift can be utilized. Such service provides the greatest fulfillment in life and the greatest blessing to others. How can one discover his gift? First, ask God. He is eager to reveal how you can best serve. Then, study the Bible to discover which gifts are given by God. Suggested chapters include Romans 12, Ephesians 4, and 1 Corinthians 12. Finally, take advantage of any opportunity that comes your way. God has a way of blessing those areas of service when we are using the talents He gives us. Often we don't know what He has given us until we try!

All believers are part of the "body of Christ" and we all need each other for the body to function properly (v.21). If one part of the body hurts, we all hurt (v.26). If we are fulfilling our role, the body is healthy. But like the Japanese sprinter, when we try to fulfill another role, we become frustrated and the cause of Christ is hindered. Let us do what we do best in the areas where God has gifted us for His Glory!

QUESTIONS:
1. What kinds of spiritual gifts are given by God?
2. Why are spiritual gifts given?
3. How has God gifted you?

ACTION POINT:

Discover your spiritual gift and use it.

Read 1 Corinthians 13:1-13

GOD'S PERFECT LOVE

And now these three remain: faith, hope and love. But the greatest of these is love.

1 Corinthians 13:13

NADIA COMANECI, a fifteen-year-old Romanian gymnast, was expected to be a tough competitor in the 1976 Olympics. But no one expected her to be perfect. Yet, the judges could find no flaws in her balance beam routine and she was awarded the first perfect score of "10" in Olympic history! But Nadia wasn't through yet. She stunned the world of sports with three more "10's" on the balance beam and then an astounding *four* more perfect marks on the uneven parallel bars! In becoming the women's all-around champion, Nadia had become world-famous for her perfect performances!

The love God has for man is even more perfect and complete than Nadia's performance in the Olympics. God's love cannot be defined, for to try to do so would detract from it. That would be like trying to define a sunset! Yet, one can *describe* love, which the Apostle Paul does in 1 Corinthians 13. He says it is better than eloquence, since lofty words without love are like clanging cymbals. Love is better than prophecy or knowledge, for a man's attitude toward someone is more important than what he knows. Love is better than faith to overcome great obstacles (v.2). To love someone is better than giving them things, since it is possible to give without loving but impossible to love without giving. Love is patient: never eager to whip others into our way of thinking of doing. Love is kind: treating others with preference and respect. Love is not envious of others, but satisfied with its God-given lot in life. Love is not boastful: always eager to tell others how great we are or what we have done. Love is not proud: carrying around an inflated ego. Love is not rude: trouncing upon the feelings of others. Love is not self-seeking: doing things out of selfish motives instead of to serve others. Love is not easily angered, but is laid back when things go against us. Love keeps no record of wrongs of others. Love delights not when evil happens, even to an enemy. Love rejoices in truth and protects others. Love is trusting instead of always regarding others with suspicion. Love hopes optimistically and perseveres when tested.

How could we ever define love? We can't. In contrast to faith, which will one day become sight, and hope, which will be fulfilled, love never ends. God's love (agapao) is more perfect than a "10" in gymnastics. He loves us because He wills to love us. If we will allow His unconditional love to flow through us, life's fragile relationships will be healed and others will be drawn to Christ.

QUESTIONS:

1. How does man's love differ from God's love?
2. Why can't we define love?
3. How would you describe love?

ACTION POINT:

Let God love others through you.

Read 1 Corinthians 15:1-58

JESUS, THE VICTOR

*For what I received I passed on to you as of first importance:
that Christ died for our sins according to the Scriptures, that
He was buried, that He was raised on the third day according
to the Scriptures.*

1 Corinthians 15:57

*But thanks be to God! He gives us the victory through our
Lord Jesus Christ.*

1 Corinthians 15:57

THE ANCIENT OLYMPIC GAMES were held in honor of
the pagan god, Zeus. A colossal forty-foot statue at Olympia
honored the "king of the gods". In his right hand stood his
daughter Nike, the goddess of victory. Supposedly, Zeus
granted success and Nike awarded the victor with the wreath
she held in her hand.

There was one victory achieved 2000 years ago that
surpasses all others in importance. And it had nothing to do
with pagan gods! *Of first importance* is the fact that Christ
died for our sins just as the Scriptures had predicted (Isa.
53). The crucifixion of Jesus, His death, and burial are
historical facts. Then He arose on the third day as the
Scriptures had predicted (Ps. 16). This is the gospel ("Good
News"). The literal, bodily resurrection of the Lord Jesus is
tremendous cause for rejoicing! To the Greeks, a bodily
resurrection ("standing up of a corpse") was unthinkable.
Yet, it was the proof of the Lordship of Jesus Christ. The
resurrection demonstrated His total victory over sin, death,
the grave, hell, and Satan.

The resurrection is the event upon which our hope is based.
The tomb of Jesus is empty! The bodies of all other religious
leaders still rest in the grave. But not Jesus' body. He is
alive today. The cowardly disciples who had deserted Him
saw Him and boldly went everywhere telling others about
the Savior. He appeared numerous times, once to a group of
over 500 people! The bodily resurrection was so well accepted
as fact that no one disputed it for years afterward!

Because He arose, we will rise to live again also! Thanks
be to God, for He passes on the victory over sin, death and

grave to all who are "in Christ" (v.22). The victory He won for us means so much more than a wreath presented by the fictitious Nike, for it is eternal. How we celebrate the victory of our King!

QUESTIONS:

1. What is the most important fact of history?
2. What would have become of Christianity if the Jews could have produced Jesus' body?
3. What enemies did Jesus destroy when He arose?

ACTION POINT:

Celebrate His Resurrection daily in your heart.

Read 2 Corinthians 2:12-17

A TRIUMPHAL PROCESSION

But thanks be to God, who always leads us in triumphal procession in Christ and through us spreads everywhere the fragrance of the knowledge of Him.

2 Corinthians 2:14

ANCIENT COMPETITORS took winning and losing very seriously. Pindar, a 5th century B.C. poet, wrote the following about the losers in wrestling at the Pythian Games in Delphi: "For them (the losers) no happy homecoming was decreed, as there was for (the victor), and as they returned to their mothers no sweet laughter brought pleasure, but they crept through the back streets, avoiding their enemies, crushed by their misfortune." This desire to win was still strong in the second century A.D. for one grave inscription of a certain Agathos Daimon read, "He died here (at Olympia) boxing in the stadium, having prayed to Zeus for the crown (of victory) or death."

If temporal victory in an athletic contest is important to athletes, how much more should the eternal victory in Christ be to children of God! That is what Paul is saying in 2 Corinthians 2:14. No matter what our external circumstances in this life, we are being led in "triumphal procession in Christ." Our lives are giving off the "smell of victory" to fellow Christians and the "smell of death" to unbelievers. Paul's choice of words compares a triumphant Roman military procession with the finished work of our glorious Lord. When a military hero achieved a total victory which ended a war and extended the boundaries of the empire, he was placed in the front of one of the grandest processions of ancient times. People crowded the streets, throwing flowers and burning incense and spices to honor the gold-robed hero as he passed by in a chariot. Spoils of war and prisoners condemned to death followed. The incense and spices were smells of victory to the Romans but smells of death to the prisoners!

Believer in Christ, you are a winner now and for eternity in life's most important battle! Because of His triumph, overwhelming victory over sin and circumstances is complete and decisive. The aroma of our victory in Christ, while sweet to Christians, becomes a convicting scent to the unbeliever, who see the effects of Jesus' victory in us (v.16). Let us remember and rejoice in what He has done!

QUESTIONS:

1. What is sweet about the Christian walk?
2. To whom is a Christian's life convicting?
3. Whom do we thank for overwhelming victory?

ACTION POINT:

Rejoice in the decisive victory won by the Lord Jesus.

Read 2 Corinthians 4:1-18

PRESSED, BUT NOT PINNED

We are hard pressed on every side, but not crushed; perplexed, but not in despair; persecuted, but not abandoned; struck down, but not destroyed.

2 Corinthians 4:8

WRESTLERS Anders Ahlgren of Sweden and Ivar Böhling of Finland were evenly matched in the light heavyweight division of the 1912 Olympics. Hour after hour they struggled, and when neither would give in after nine hours, officials finally called the match a draw! Both were declared co-winners and were the top finishers in the event. Each had been hard-pressed, but never pinned!

Sometimes our Christian lives seem like the wrestling match between Ahlgren and Böhling. We are hard pressed by Satan and circumstances, almost to the point of despair. The struggle goes on and on, beyond the "time limit" we would have set. Yet, though the struggle is intense, we always overcome by the power of God! We are never abandoned by Him, never need to despair, and are never really crushed or destroyed! Unlike the competitors in the Olympic wrestling match, we never need to settle for a draw! We are *more than winners* through Him who loved us!

Christian friend, never lose heart. Remember, your troubles are light and momentary compared to the eternal glory ahead (v.17). Fix your eyes on the eternal, unseen God and you will be renewed inwardly day by day.

QUESTIONS:
1. What circumstance tends to "get you down"?
2. How does the Lord give you victory over it?
3. Why are we able to continue with courage?

ACTION POINT:

Remember to dwell on the things that are eternal.

45

Read 2 Corinthians 5:1-10

THE WINNER'S CIRCLE

So we make it our goal to please Him, whether we are at home in the body or away from it. For we must all appear before the judgment seat of Christ, that each one may receive what is due him for the things done while in the body, whether good or bad.

2 Corinthians 5:9-10

DURING THE HEIGHT of their empire, the Greeks placed a high premium on winning in athletic competitions. While the losers were virtually ignored, the winners were escorted before a box seat called the "bema". There sat the commissioner of the games. As the winner approached, he was presented a victory wreath in a glamorous and noble ceremony.

While unbelievers are destined to be judged at the Great White Throne (Rev.20:11-15), all those who are saved by God's grace will one day stand before the "bema" of the Lord Jesus Christ. This judgment is not to determine whether Christians will be saved in Heaven or lost in hell, for the salvation of all who trust Christ is already guaranteed (John 6:37-40, 10:28). This "ceremony" is for the purpose of awarding or denying "crowns" to Christians for faithfulness to God in this life! Such a judgment is alarming enough to the child of God! Every opportunity God has given us to glorify Him in thought, word, and deed will be considered. And God is very impartial. He knows what time, talent, and treasure He has given us in this life. He knows the motive behind every action we have taken! And He will reward accordingly.

We must be "wise builders" in this life, for the Lord will test our works with fire (1 Cor. 3:10-15). How tragic to lose the rewards we might have enjoyed had we lived entirely for Him! How wonderful to be rewarded with one of the five crowns mentioned in Scripture! There is the Imperishable Crown (1 Cor. 9:24-27) given for self discipline: the Crown of Rejoicing (1 Thess. 2:19) given for sowing good seed in the lives of others: the Crown of Life (James 1:12, Rev. 2:10) given for enduring trials for Christ's sake; the Crown of

Righteousness (2 Tim. 4:8) given for living in purity while looking forward to His coming again; and the Crown of Glory (1 Pet. 5:4) given for leadership of God's people.

Can you visualize standing before the "box seat" of Jesus Christ, the Commissioner of the Game of Life? What prizes will He be able to present to you? If you spend your life giving, loving, and serving Him by the power of His Spirit, your rewards will be great.

QUESTIONS:
1. Who will appear before Christ's judgment seat?
2. What will His judgment be based upon?
3. How will you feel when you stand before Him?

ACTION POINT:

Live so that the Lord Jesus may reward you well.

Read 2 Corinthians 5:11-21

AN ATHLETIC
AMBASSADOR

We are therefore Christ's ambassadors, as though God were making His appeal through us. We implore you on Christ's behalf: be reconciled to God.

2 Corinthians 5:20

POLE VAULTER FRED HANSEN, representing the United States, dueled Wolfgang Reinhardt of Germany in a long, drawn out battle in the 1964 Olympic Games. The final lasted 8 3/4 hours, and when he finally won the gold medal, Hansen had this to say: "Please don't think I'm corny, but I was thinking what I could do for my country, not for myself." The young American from Cuero, Texas, had not only upheld a winning tradition in the pole vault (the USA had never lost in the regular Olympics), but he also had proven himself to be a great ambassador for his country. Like any good ambassador, Hansen put the country's reputation ahead of his own.

Christians are ambassadors to a strange world for their living Lord of Glory. The question is, "What kind of ambassadors are we?" Like Fred Hansen, we must not be living for self. We must live for the Lord Jesus, who died for us and was raised again (v. 15). We are a "new creation in Christ (v. 17)" and God has given us a "ministry" of showing and telling the world that God loves fallen man and is reconciled to every man who is in Christ! Whenever a person will be reconciled to God, he is saved! This is our message! We must be faithful to encourage others to accept this gracious gift. The very love of Christ motivates us to share the good news (v.14)!

As Fred Hansen did not compete for himself in the Olympic pole vault, we must not live life for ourselves. Our lives are far too useful and important to our loving Lord Jesus to waste pursuing selfish interests. Let us be good ambassadors for Christ, only doing and saying those things which bring glory to Him. Then, when He calls us home, the Lord Jesus will be able to say, "Well done!"

48

QUESTIONS:

1. What is the responsibility of an ambassador?
2. Who is an ambassador for Christ?
3. What is the compelling force to share Christ?

ACTION POINT:

Live and speak as a representative of Heaven on this earth.

Read 2 Corinthians 6:14-18

SAME COACH, SAME GOALS

Do not be yoked together with unbelievers. For what do righteousness and wickedness have in common? Or what fellowship can light have with darkness?

2 Corinthians 6:14

THE COMMITMENT to a cause greater than self is a prerequisite for success in any team sport. All members of a team must be dedicated to the same coach and to the achievement of the same goal, or there will be disharmony and the effort of the team will be hindered. An Old Testament prophet pointed out this need for unity in mind and purpose when he wrote that two cannot even walk together unless they are agreed beforehand (Amos 3:3).

As children of the Heavenly Father, we are given explicit directions for many of our relationships. When we obey God's instructions, our lives are blessed and the Christian team prospers. The Lord knows that when we live and work closely with someone and when shared responsibility is involved, both parties must be of one mind. Since the world's way of doing things is always the antitheses of God's way (Is. 55:8-9), we are not to be "unequally yoked together with unbelievers " (v. 14). This word picture portrays an old law against yoking a donkey and an ox together to pull a cart or a plow (Deut. 22:10). How difficult (if not impossible) such a practice would be! It would be cruel to both animals!

While God does not want us to shun unbelievers, much sorrow could be avoided if Christians would plan no deep, sympathetic union of mind and will with them. This applies to relationships which involve both as equals in responsibility and authority. Though God loves all, those who refuse to accept Christ remain children of the Devil (John 8:42-47). Someone has warned, "a Christian who marries an unbeliever is bound to have trouble with his father-in-law (not the earthly one either!)." Business partnerships and other unions where one's partner does not trust the Lord Jesus must also be avoided. While God does not prohibit working under or over unsaved individuals, He is very specific about relationships which bind people together on equal footing.

God will always be a loving Heavenly Father to his children. He desires to direct every relationship for our good and for His glory. The holiness and purity of Christ has nothing in common with the wickedness and impurity of Satan's kingdom. We will be far happier if we only "team up" with those who love Jesus and are committed to serving the Master Coach.

QUESTIONS:
1. Why is it good policy not to date unbelievers?
2. What harmony can light have with darkness?
3. How else can you apply 2 Corinthians 6:14?

ACTION POINT:

Never join an unbeliever in a close relationship.

Read 2 Corinthians 9:6-15

GENEROUS GIVING

. . . Whoever sows sparingly will also reap sparingly, and whoever sows generously will also reap generously. Each man should give what he has decided in his heart to give, not reluctantly or under compulsion, for God loves a cheerful giver.

2 Corinthians 9:6-7

EMIL ZATOPEK of Czechoslovakia left an indelible impression on the world of sports because of the effort that he gave and the attitude with which be gave it. He appeared in three Olympics ('48,'52, and '56) and is best remembered for his 1952 victories in the 5,000 meters, the 10,000 meters and finally in the marathon — which he had never run before! Fearful of not running at the right pace, Zatopek ran alongside favorite Jim Peters of Great Britain. After 15 kilometers at a torrid pace, Emil asked whether the pace was good enough. The exhausted Peters lied, telling him it was too slow! Soon Zatopek shot on past, finishing the 26 miles in 2:23:03.2, a new Olympic record! Though winning convincingly, Zatopek later said, "I was unable to walk for a whole week after that, so much did the race take out of me. But it was the most pleasant exhaustion I have ever known." Emil Zatopek gave much more to his country than four gold medals and 18 world records. And his attitude won friends from among fellow competitors and countrymen alike.

God wants us to give to others with the same attitude that Emil Zatopek had in giving to his country. He loves to see us giving joyfully of our time, talent and treasure. Though we are not under any Old Testament law to tithe, with the proper attitude Christians will want to give far beyond the percentage required of Israel before Christ came. In following the principle of generosity outlined in 2 Corinthians 9:6-15, we will be blessed by God. While we should not give to get, if we give to God He has promised to reward us. He gives us more "seed" so we can give more (v.10)! Certainly we should sow our gifts wisely in God's kingdom. If we give time in teaching others, it should be quality time of Bible study with practical application and not a discussion of man's opinion. If we give talent, it should be as unto God and in a way that draws others to praise and worship Him. If we give money, it should be to ministries that honor God's inerrant Word, share the Gospel of Christ boldly and are willing to be accountable for how funds are handled.

As Emil Zatopek gave willingly and joyfully to his country, God wants us to give in the same manner. If we are giving grudgingly or under compulsion (v.7), we may as well stop. Our Lord will be pleased and His kingdom advanced by generous givers who give because of a deep desire to honor Him by their gifts.

QUESTIONS:
1. What is the proper motive for giving?
2. How does God reward generous giving?
3. What is God's indescribable gift (v.15)?

ACTION POINT:

Give to God with a joyful attitude.

Read Galatians 2:17-21

MAN'S POWER SHORTAGE

I have been crucified with Christ and I no longer live, but Christ lives in me. The life I live in the body, I live by faith in the Son of God, who loved me and gave Himself for me.
Galatians 2:20

ENGLISH RUNNER Jim Peters had a tremendous two-mile lead as he entered the stadium to run the last leg of the 26-mile marathon in the 1954 British Commonwealth games. But 200 yards from the finish line his confident smile faded and he staggered and fell to the ground. Peters tried to crawl, but failed miserably. Exhaustion had taken its toll and he couldn't move an inch! Another runner soon passed him and was declared the winner.

If only a fresh runner could have entered Jim Peters' body, he could have won the Marathon in 1954. But everyone knows that is not physically possible. Yet, that's exactly what happens spiritually when a person accepts Jesus Christ! The Spirit of God indwells a believer to give power for living! As God sees it, we are positionally dead, crucified with Christ! We are dead to the requirements of trying to keep the law, for we can't do it because of a "power shortage." We are dead to our own selfish interests, plans and goals. The power of the risen Christ now resides within us to energize us to finish the race! He is on the throne. His interests, plans and goals for us (Rom. 8:29) are all that matter now.

His power is realized in us experientially as we trust Him by faith. We should not seek to crucify self, for we cannot do it anyway. It is an accomplished fact with continuing implications as we rest in God's grace. God has given us a salvation for which we did not and can not work and which we do not deserve. That's the essence of grace. There is no other way of salvation and there is no other way of living in victory as a Christian (v.21).

Next time you feel like Jim Peters, unable to continue in the race of life, remember who Christ is and that He dwells within you. Though your own power is insufficient, His power is without limit. He who made you a winner in Christ will empower you to live as you trust Him by faith.

QUESTIONS:

1. What does it mean to be crucified with Christ?
2. Who lives within a believer?
3. How is the life of Christ lived through us?

ACTION POINT:

Trust God by faith to live through you.

Read Galatians 5:1-12

HINDRANCE ON THE TRACK

You were running a good race. Who cut in on you and kept you from obeying the truth?

Galatians 5:7

THE OPENING ROUND of the 1500-meter race in the 1972 Munich Olympics featured a showdown between defending champions Kip Keino of Kenya and Jim Ryun of the USA. Though Ryun had come out of retirement, the fourth heat was to prove the end of his amateur career. Boxed in 550 meters from the finish, Ryun tried to squeeze between two runners rather than pass on the outside. Suddenly Vitus Ashaba of Uganda moved right into the path of Ryun, causing the American to trip on his heel and fall to the track. Ryun landed on the curb with a bruised hip, scraped knee, sprained ankle and a concussion to his Adam's apple. Despite the cheers from a sympathetic crowd, Ryun had lost too much valuable time and couldn't catch up. "All I know is everything was going well and I felt good, and the next thing I knew I was trying to figure out what happened," he said.

Religious legalists (Judaizers) caused an equally disastrous collision in the lives of new Christians in Galatia during Paul's ministry. He wrote the book of Galatians to tell them: "It is for freedom that Christ has set us free (5:1)!" The people had been "running well," following Jesus by grace through faith and depending on the still, small voice of His Spirit to lead them. Legalists had slipped into the church and caused the people to "break stride." They didn't dispute everything, but added certain works (circumcision) as a condition for salvation. Paul confronted this heresy by asking, "Who cut in on you? (v.7)". He knew that if *any* works are added to the gospel of grace as a condition for being saved, the whole principle of grace is destroyed (Rom.11:6, 4:5). Mixing grace and works is like mixing oil and water. Man is saved simply by believing and we can *do* nothing to keep our salvation!

Salvation comes only when we trust Christ and do nothing else, for He did all the work necessary! Baptism, church

56

membership and giving money are all good works, but they are never required as a condition for salvation. Even after we are saved, no one can place man-made rules upon us as measures of spirituality. To live by rules is to fall from the grace way of living (v.4) and lose the joy of our Christian life. A winner in Christ is free to please God by loving obedience to God's word and not man's rules.

QUESTIONS:
1. Why did Paul write to the Galatians?
2. How do legalists trip up believers today?
3. Why do grace and works not mix?

ACTION POINT:

Follow Christ by grace through faith.

Read Galatians 5:13-26

CONFLICT AND
THE FRUIT OF VICTORY

So I say, live by the Spirit, and you will not gratify the desires of the sinful nature.

Galatians 5:16

But the fruit of the Spirit is love, joy, peace, patience, kindness, goodness, faithfulness, gentleness and self-control.

Galatians 5:22-23

Since we live by the Spirit, let us keep in step with the Spirit.

Galatians 5:25

IN THE SUPER HEAVYWEIGHT division of the 1964 Tokyo Olympic weightlifting competition, 341-pound Leonid Zhabotinsky of the Soviet Union lulled his own teammate, Yury Vlassov, into a false sense of security by conceding defeat before the event was concluded. Zhabotinsky then scored a major upset over the favored Vlassov by setting a world record in the jerk on his final attempt. Vlassov was furious over the dishonest trick by his teammate. "I was choked with tears," he said. "I flung the silver medal through the window. I had always revered the purity, the impartiality of contests of strength. That night I understood that there is a kind of strength that has nothing to do with justice.

Just as there was internal conflict and deceit within the Soviet weightlifting team, there is an inner conflict in the life of every believer. Even though all who have trusted are winners *positionally* in Him, *experientially* we are not yet perfect. In fact, because of the war between our old sin nature (flesh) and our new nature (spirit) given us by God, we can expect a constant battle for control of our actions until physical death (v.17). That is why Paul writes that "since we live by the Spirit, we should walk by the Spirit"(v.25). Our life is like a war between two countries. An outside force (Jesus) has stepped in and won the war. The losing side (the flesh) uses guerrilla tactics to continue the fight in spite of the fact that the final outcome was secured at Calvary. The

58

flesh still raises its ugly head and causes us to sin when we allow it.

What is the key to victory over sin? How can our *practice* more closely resemble our *position* in Christ? We need simply to let the Spirit control us by faith and not by obeying a list of laws. We are never told to live a "good life" by our own efforts, but simply to "live by the Spirit" (v.16). As God's Holy Spirit controls us, we enjoy the sweet fruit of victory: love for others, genuine joy, patience in adversity, kindness towards others, goodness (clear-cut honesty), faithfulness (reliability), gentleness (humility), and self-control (self-discipline).

You are a winner in Christ! But the flesh will still wage guerrilla warfare to prevent you from living God's way. Only by walking in the power of God's Spirit can you demonstrate the characteristics of a winner in Christ.

QUESTIONS:

1. What is the power that enables you to live a Christian life?
2. Why is there an internal war in a believer's life?
3. What are the keys to representing Christ?

ACTION POINT:

By faith, walk in the power of God's Spirit.

Read Galatians 6:7-18

LAW OF THE HARVEST

Do not be deceived: God cannot be mocked. A man reaps what he sows.

Galatians 6:7

THE FENCING TOURNAMENT of the pentathlon in the 1976 Montreal Olympics was laden with controversy when Soviet Army Major Boris Onischenko, the defending silver medalist, seemed to be able to register a hit against two opponents without even touching them. When his sword was examined, it was discovered that Onischenko had illegally wired it with a hidden push-button circuit breaker in a desperate quest for victory. He was taken away from the Olympic village almost immediately and was never seen outside Russia again!

The fate of the Soviet swordsman illustrates an unchangeable law of the universe; man reaps what he sows. This "law of the harvest" involves three principles. First, one reaps the *same* crop that he sows. No farmer ever sowed wheat and reaped cotton. Every wheat kernel produces wheat. Similarly, sexual sin produces psychological suffering and disease (VD and AIDS), outbursts of anger produce murder and prison terms, and selfish sins produce alienated friendships and frustration. On the other hand, marital fidelity produces a happy and healthy home, self-control produces an atmosphere of peace and goodwill, and generosity produces close friendships and prosperity (Luke 6:38). *What goes around comes around!*

Second, one always reaps *much more* than he sows. One kernel of wheat produces dozens more and one kernel of corn produces hundreds. It is futile to sow wild oats and then pray for a crop failure! Therefore, we must be all the more careful about the kinds of seed we sow!

Finally, the harvest comes *after* the sowing. We need not become discouraged if it seems long in coming. Wheat has been found in Egyptian tombs that was placed there 5,000 years ago. When planted it still produced wheat! God cannot be mocked. The literal meaning of this verse is, "you cannot turn your nose up at God."

The question is not "Am I going to sow today?" but "What am I going to sow today?" Like planted seed, every deed goes out of sight temporarily. But the harvest is sure and will one day be evident to all.

QUESTIONS:
1. To whom are we to be especially good (v.10)?
2. What have you reaped regretfully?
3. What have you reaped with joy?

ACTION POINT:

Sow good seeds by the Spirit of God.

Read Ephesians 1:1-23

THE VICTORY PLATFORM

Praise be to the God and Father of our Lord Jesus Christ who has blessed us in the heavenly realms with every spiritual blessing in Christ.

Ephesians 1:3

WHILE THE LOSERS were virtually ignored, the winners of the ancient Greek Olympic games were greatly revered by their states. Though he received only a wreath at the site of the games (1 Cor. 9:26), when the victor returned to his home city it was entirely different. First, they punched a hole in the city wall through which they entered. This hole was then covered by a plaque with his name on it. He was given a ticker-tape parade in a gold chariot and a statue was erected in his honor. He not only received a box seat at future Isthmian games, but he also received a cash award of 10,000 drachma and was tax exempt for life. His family was fed at public expense for life and his children were educated by the state. Clearly, the Greeks loved their winners!

The heavenly Father loves His winners even more than the Greeks loved theirs, for He has blessed us in our "home city" (heaven) with "every spiritual blessing in Christ." Though earthly rewards may seem few and far between, our spiritual heritage is "out of this world." We have *grace* and *peace* (v.2), and we are chosen to be *holy* and *blameless* before Him (v.4). He has predestined us to *adoption* as sons (v.5). We have *redemption* and *forgiveness* (v.7). Christ and His purpose are made *known* to us (v.9) and we are *sealed* with the Holy Spirit (v.13) which guarantees our inheritance (v.14). Heaven and all of God's blessings are assured. Even the Greeks couldn't treat their winners that well!

Next time discouragement threatens, remember that you are an eternal winner in Christ. The rewards on earth may come and go, but God's blessings in the heavenly realm remain constant!

QUESTIONS:

1. Who has made you a winner?
2. Who deserves all the praise?
3. How are heavenly blessings related to earthly benefits?

ACTION POINT:

Thank and praise God for His abundant blessings.

Read Ephesians 2:1-10

TROPHIES OF HIS GRACE

For it is by grace you have been saved, through faith - and this not from yourselves, it is the gift of God — not by works, so that no one can boast.

Ephesians 2:8-9

PART OF THE OLYMPIC ideal is that each nation displays its outstanding amateur athletes. On opening day, all the athletes parade past the spectators, each nation's contestants dressed alike and following the flag of his homeland. Every athlete is a hero to his home country, a "trophy" representing the best that nation has to offer.

The trophies that God displays are redeemed people purchased with the blood of the Lord Jesus Christ! When we trust Him as Savior, He saves us by His mercy and grace. Our destiny is to be forever displayed before the universe as objects of His grace (v.7). That is the point of Ephesians 2:1-10. While verses 1-3 of Ephesians 2 are as black as they can be (revealing our past character and position), verses 4-10 are as bright as can be (revealing our present position in Christ). This salvation in Christ is a gift for which we do not (and can not) work. If we worked for our salvation it would not be by grace (Rom. 11:6). If we are relying on anything other than God's grace to be saved, we are lost because we can never do enough works to merit Heaven! That's why there will be no boasting in Heaven, for none of us will have anything to boast about!

This is opposed to the idea of "religion". Religion is man doing the work and man claiming the credit. Christianity (salvation) is God doing the work in the sacrifice of Christ and God getting credit. Religion is man trying to please God (which is impossible). Salvation is man coming helplessly to God by faith. Religion is a system of rules and rituals. Salvation is a relationship with the living God made possible through His grace. Finally, religion is self *doing* something, while salvation is *being* something in Christ. Jesus did not say, "I have come that you might have religion." He said, "I have come that you might have life" (John 10:10).

We are born again when we are made alive in Christ (v.4) and then we are seated positionally in heavenly places (v.6). This eternal position will be reflected in our experience (v.10). God has us on display as trophies of His grace toward undeserving sinners, that He may be eternally praised!

QUESTIONS:
1. What is man's natural condition?
2. How does salvation through grace change man's position?
3. Why does God reach down and save us?

ACTION POINT:

Live in thanksgiving and praise to God for His grace to you.

Read Ephesians 3:14-21

POWER ON THE INSIDE

I pray that out of His glorious riches He may strengthen you with power through His Spirit in your inner being, so that Christ may dwell in your hearts through faith. And I pray that you . . . may have power . . . to grasp how wide and long and high and deep is the love of Christ and to know this love that surpasses knowledge.

Ephesians 3:16-19

THE GREATEST WEIGHT ever lifted by a human being was 6,270 pounds in a back lift (raised off trestles) by a 364-pound Paul Anderson, the 1956 Olympic heavyweight champion from Toccoa, Georgia, on June 12, 1957. It was an awesome sight as Anderson, a devout Christian, lifted over three tons that day! By comparison, the heaviest Rolls Royce (the Phantom VI) weighs 5,600 pounds!

We are in awe of such physical power and yet we often find ourselves becoming so weak and faint-hearted on the inside. This was the point of Paul's prayer for the Ephesians. Because of the greatness of God's plan to save us and because of our unchanging position in Christ, Paul prays that by God's power (Gk. dunamis: "dynamic living power") we might be strengthened inside and that Christ may dwell deeply ("be at home and in total authority:) in our hearts through faith. Furthermore, Paul prays that we may be able to comprehend not only how *wide* Christ's love reaches (to everyone), but also it's *length* (from the foundation of the world through eternity), its *height* (how high He takes us) and its *depth* (how deep it reaches into the inner man). What great love! We love *some* people *some* of the time and to a limited degree. But God's love is infinite. He loves all men, all of the time, and to an infinite degree! Only by dwelling in His love and being strengthened with His power can we avoid discouragement in the external circumstances of life (v.13). Yet, because He is able to do "immeasurably more then all we ask for or imagine," we are empowered to live above circumstances and to function as "more than winners" in Christ Jesus!

Though not all of us are as strong as Paul Anderson in realizing the great love of Christ, everyone can be strengthened with an inner power through the Spirit of God. This supernatural power is even more awesome, as it carries us above and beyond the most difficult circumstances of life!

QUESTIONS:
1. What position did Paul assume in prayer?
2. What does Paul ask of Christians who read his letter?
3. How is it possible to know the love of Christ?

ACTION POINT:

If Christ is a Resident on your life, make Him President as well.

Read Ephesians 4:17-24

CURE FOR CALLOUSNESS

... you must no longer live as the Gentiles do, in the futility of their thinking. They are darkened in their understanding and separated from the life of God because of the ignorance that is in them due to the hardening of their hearts. Having lost all sensitivity, they have given themselves over to sensuality...

Ephesians 4:17-19

SINCE WE ARE WINNERS in Christ, we are not to live as unbelievers live (v.17). How do unbelievers live? Well, because of the hardness (callousness) of their hearts (v.18) they have lost sensitivity to God's gentle Spirit (v.19). They indulge in all kinds of sin in thought and deed, and they have a greedy desire for more impurity. The unbeliever's heart resembles the baseball pitcher who develops a "hot spot" where a seam of the ball rubs when he throws a curve. Eventually a blister forms and hardens into a callous making him insensitive to the feel of the ball. Only the removal of the blister by surgery can restore his sensitivity. In the same manner it takes God's surgery, spiritual rebirth of the heart, to remove sin and the desire for impurity.

The first sin to put off is lying (v.25). Satan is a liar and the father of all lies. Not only must we not lie, but we must also speak the entire truth. Second, we must abandon all but righteous anger. In some cases it is wrong not to be angry with sin. But even our justified anger must be controlled. Satan loves to see anger increase unduly and lead us into sin. Third, we must work honestly. A believer should give a day's work for a day's pay. Work is encouraged in Scripture, for if we earn an income we can help others.

What is your condition today? Are you sensitive to the leadership of the Spirit of God? Or, because of callousness, will God need to perform spiritual surgery on your heart? Let this reminder of who you are in Christ soften your heart so you will hear Him speak.

QUESTIONS:

1. What are characteristics of a lost person?
2. How is a believer in Christ to be different?
3. What sins must you put off?

ACTION POINT:

Be sensitive to the voice of God's Spirit.

Read Ephesians 4:25-5:21

THE POWER OF WORDS

Do not let any unwholesome talk come out of your mouth, but only what is helpful for building others up according to their needs, that it may benefit those who listen.

Ephesians 4:29

THE POWER of a coach's word prior to an athletic contest has never been more visibly demonstrated than before the 1980 USA-Russian Olympic hockey game at Lake Placid, New York. American coach Herb Brooks, a famed disciplinarian, told his young team, "Gentlemen, you don't have enough talent to win on talent alone." Nevertheless, on the morning of the match, Brooks challenged them by saying, "You're born to be a player. You're meant to be here. This moment is yours. You're meant to be here at this time." With those words, the Americans fought and scrapped, played "above their heads" and scored an emotional upset over the world's dominant hockey team!

A winning Christian life is also demonstrated by the power of words. For this reason, Paul reminds us to only utter helpful words to build up others. All unwholesome (literal, "rotten") words (v.29), obscenity (shameless talk and conduct), foolish talk (meaningless chatter) and coarse jesting (vulgar, frivolous wit) must go (5:4). We must resist the temptation to use suggestive words, innuendos, and stories loaded with double meanings to "get a laugh". While humor itself is great, it is wrong to use humor to tear others down. We must be careful to refrain from discussing the sins of others openly, for dwelling upon evil is shameful (5:12).

How is speaking like a winner in Christ possible? Only by being filled continually with the Holy Spirit of God (5:18) and by being thankful for everything (5:20). It is God, through the Spirit's power, who works through our mouths to transform our words for His glory!

QUESTIONS:

1. How is controlling the tongue possible?
2. What should be our purpose in speaking?
3. Why is avoiding an innuendo difficult?

ACTION POINT:

Build another person up with your words.

Read Ephesians 6:10-18

GOD'S UNIFORM

Put on the full armor of God so that you can take your stand against the devil's schemes.

Ephesians 6:11

AMERICAN FOOTBALL has always been a sport of violent physical contact. In 1905 Swarthmore had a talented big man named Box Maxwell when they took on Penn in a key contest. Knowing they had a better chance of victory if they could get Maxwell out of the game, Penn players gave him a physical pounding. In those days, helmets and pads were of very poor quality. Box stumbled off of the field. Newspapers later carried photos of his battered face, prompting President Theodore Roosevelt to threaten to abolish football if rough play was not eliminated.

Since the Garden of Eden, believers in Jesus have faced an enemy more deadly and hateful than any opponent on any football field (1 Pet. 5:8-9). His name is Satan or Lucifer and he hated mankind because he hates the God who loves us. Jesus recognized Satan's kingdom in Matthew 12:26. The Lord created us to love and to glorify Himself, but Satan would try to rob God of that glory by drawing our service to himself. Satan is subtle, powerful, and experienced. He has over 7,000 years of practice in seducing mankind since Adam and Eve. Though God will eventually abolish Satan's rough play, that day has not yet come. His weapons abound in the demonic kingdom around us. He magnifies our desires and uses the peer pressure of the world to tempt us to sin. He is organized and he is ruthless. There are demons who oversee nations, manipulate businesses, and even control religious groups. Without God's armor we are no match for him. But God has given us both a uniform and weapons with which we can stand firm and fight him off!

What is included in the Christian's armor? As Paul described our "uniform," he probably was observing a Roman soldier on guard duty. The soldier's belt held every other part of the uniform in place. The Lord gives us a "belt of truth" - personal integrity to stand for what is right. Christ's righteousness is our breastplate, capable of

72

withstanding any blow from Satan. The "helmet of salvation" strengthens our minds and enables us to "reason together with Him" (Isa. 1:18). We stand firm on feet shod with the Gospel of peace.

Our armor also includes offensive weapons. God's Word is the word of the Spirit. The Word is a powerful weapon (Heb. 4:12) which Jesus himself used (Matt. 4:1-11). Our prayers and supplications (specific requests) are also powerful and cannot be overcome by Satan!

Though spiritually seated forever in heavenly places (Eph. 2:6), we walk physically in the world. We overcome only in the power of His might (v.10). There is no protection on the back side, so retreat is impossible. Let us stand in His mighty power!

QUESTIONS:
1. Where did Paul get the idea of the armor of God?
2. How does Satan attack you?
3. How did Jesus frustrate the devil?

ACTION POINT:

Make use of God's armor this week.

Read Philippians 1:1-30

WINNERS EITHER WAY

For to me, to live is Christ and to die is gain.

Philippians 1:21

AFTER EIGHT of the ten events of the 1976 Montreal Olympic decathlon were concluded, it was evident that Bruce Jenner was assured of victory. He began crying when he realized his long-sought goal was achieved. No matter how he ran the remaining races, he was the winner. Though most athletes dreaded the final 1500-meter race, Bruce ran it enthusiastically, finishing full of strength to the delight of the crowd. He had set a new world record (8,617 points) bettering his old personal best by 94 points!

No matter what happens to the believer, from the time he trusts Christ to save him he is an eternal winner. By God's grace, we will one day be just like Jesus! God's continued work in us assures it (v.6). Paul, in writing to the Philippians from a prison cell where his life was in imminent danger, recognized that for him to live would be to exalt Christ on earth (v.21). His life found all meaning in Christ! But to die meant gain (v.21), for he would then be with Jesus, glorifying Him in heaven! Being in somewhat of a dilemma, Paul left the matter with God (as if he had a choice!). In verse 23, he stated that he desired to depart and he used a military term meaning "to take up one's tent and to move on." Yet he felt confident that he would be living longer for the good of others (v.25). His attitude was "either way, Lord, I will rejoice in whatever you choose, for by grace you have given me victory." Paul was not indifferent to his fate, but only concerned that Christ be exalted. Therefore, like Bruce Jenner, he could run the last leg of his race with determination and assurance.

God works in all believers "to will and to act according to His good purpose (Phil. 2:13)". As a Christian, do you accept with rejoicing the plan of God for you? Whether we live or die, the essential thing is that Christ be exalted. With final victory assured, let us run with great patience the race set before us (Heb. 12:1).

QUESTIONS:

1. What was Paul's attitude toward imprisonment?
2. What was Paul's attitude toward life and death?
3. In addition to believing in Christ, what is the privilege given to believers (v.29)?

ACTION POINT:

Rejoice in all your suffering.

Read Philippians 2:1-18

HUMILITY AND HONOR

Your attitude should be the same as that of Christ Jesus.
Philippians 2:5

THE 1964 OLYMPIC VICTORY of Great Britain's Anthony Nash and Robin Dixon in the two-man bobsled race can be attributed to Italian Eugenio Monti, an eight-time world champion himself. When the British duo prepared for their second run, they noticed a broken axle bolt on their sled. Monti saw their problem, removed a bolt from his own sled, and gave it to them. This self-sacrifice allowed the Nash-Dixon team to win and prevented Monti from achieving his dream of an Olympic gold medal. Eugenio Monti had to wait until 1968, when he finally won and Olympic gold as a 40 year-old man in Grenoble, France.

Monti's humility is the attitude about which Paul wrote to the Philippians. This self-sacrifice, as opposed to selfish ambition (v.3), which was a great enemy of the early Church, was the attitude of our Lord Jesus. The Master voluntarily humbled Himself and took on the restriction of a body when He came to Earth as the God-man. With no fear of losing His deity, He joyfully forsook the glory of Heaven in the interest of others. He became a humble carpenter in an insignificant town, lived unselfishly, and died the most ignominious death possible at the hands of the Romans, for crucifixion was reserved for only the worst of criminals. Therefore (v.9), the Father has exalted Him above every other name! One day everyone will recognize His Lordship, though it will be too late for the salvation of those in Hell!

Believers are to demonstrate His attitude not by imitating Him in their own power, but by the power of the Holy Spirit. We are to work *out* (not work *for*) the salvation (v.12) that God has worked *in* us. A spirit of pride in dealing with others indicates a lack of humility before God. God approves those who have a humble heart (Isa.66:2) and will one day exalt them (Matt. 23:12).

QUESTIONS:

1. Where does the power to be humble originate?
2. Why did Jesus humble himself?
3. Who will one day admit that Jesus is Lord?

ACTION POINT:

Let your salvation be known by humility.

Read Philippians 3:1-21

A SINGLE GOAL

But one thing I do: Forgetting what is behind and straining toward what is ahead, I press on toward the goal to win the prize for which God has called me heavenward in Christ Jesus.

Philippians 3:13-14

A SEVENTEEN-YEAR-OLD pixie from the Soviet Union captured the imagination of the United States for her performance in women's gymnastics during the 1972 Munich Olympics. Olga Korbut, 4 foot 11 inches tall and weighing 85 pounds, had qualified for her team as an alternate and was only allowed to compete when a teammate was injured. She soon caught the eye of the crowd for a spectacular routine on the uneven parallel bars and it seemed that she even had a chance for the All - Around championship. But disaster struck as she performed poorly the next day. Scoring only a 7.5 on the uneven parallels, she wept in disappointment. The following day, before millions of people, she regained her composure and her form. Olga finished second on the uneven parallel bars and won the gold medal for balance beam and floor exercise routine. Her persistence as she "pressed on for the prize" won the hearts of American Olympic fans.

Olga Korbut's single-minded persistence is the type that Paul wrote about in Philippians three. He said that his one goal was to forget the past and press on toward the goal that God had for him. In verses 1-11, the apostle revealed that he used to take great pride in his self-righteousness and human effort to please God. But now, with no confidence whatever in his own achievements (v.9), his over-riding goal became to know Christ more intimately and to become like Jesus (Rom. 8:29). Doing this required single-mindedness, a willingness to forget the past, and the drive to press on. Though Paul "knew" Christ (v. 8), had been saved for 30 years, and was assured of heaven, he wasn't perfect yet. He wanted to "know" Christ by experience (v.10), and was looking to the heavenly rewards God would give him for faithfulness while on earth.

78

Since none of us has spiritually "arrived" either, we need the same determination shown by the apostle Paul and later by Olga Korbut. Whether yesterday has been filled with success or failure, we must not dwell upon the past. Let us press on, trusting God to produce Christ's likeness in us. The only goal we need is to become like Jesus in every thought, word and deed.

QUESTIONS:

1. What is your chief goal in life?
2. Why must we forget the past?
3. How is the character of Jesus produced in us?

ACTION POINT:

Become single-minded in your goal to know Christ.

Read Philippians 4:1-23

MIND OF A WINNER

Finally, brothers, whatever is true, whatever is noble (worthy of respect), whatever is right, whatever is pure, whatever is lovely (winsome), whatever is admirable —if anything is excellent or praiseworthy — think about such things.

Philippians 4:8

WHEN HE WAS in junior high school, Jim Ryun was told by his track coach that he probably should try another sport. Instead, he arose every morning at 4:30 A.M. and ran six miles before breakfast. Then he ran six more miles after school. Jim refused to dwell on the negative and at age 17 he became the first high school boy to run a four-minute mile. Later he ran a world record 3:51:3! Ryun possessed the positive mind set of a champion.

Not only did the apostle Paul possess the same mind set, but he also admonished all other believers to think like winners! We are commanded to rejoice in the Lord always (v.4). This is a realistic expectation because the basis of our joy is the Lord and not outward circumstances. This inner joy which is not based upon position, wealth or achievements, drives out discord and always produces harmony. Next, we are to let the gentleness in our lives be evident (v.5). Winners in Christ are to have no anxiety about anything, but to pray about everything (v. 6). Prayer is the great antidote for worry, for it is impossible to do both simultaneously. Someone has aptly stated that worry is "trust in the devil." Put another way, worry is like racing a car's engine when the transmission is in neutral. We are *never* to worry, but always to pray about everything, knowing that God cared about the smallest problems in our lives. In fact, to an omnipotent God, all problems are small!

Finally, the mind of winning Christians is to be set on the true, noble, right, pure, lovely, admirable, excellent, and the praiseworthy. This means turning away from the world's negative influences and fixing our minds upon Jesus, who is all of these things.

As winners in Christ, let us take a tip from this great chapter on mental health. Dwell on the positive! Such a mind set produces great contentment (v.13) and the peace of God will guard ("garrison") our hearts and minds (v. 7). His peace is far superior to our schemes about how things should work out.

QUESTIONS:
1. What influences must you avoid to think like a winner?
2. What influences should you seek in thinking like a winner?
3. What are the results of a positive mind set?

ACTION POINT:

Discipline your mind to think positively.

Read Colossians 1:1-23

THE REAL "NUMBER ONE"

He is the image of the invisible God, the firstborn over all creation. For by Him all things were created: things in heaven and on earth, visible and invisible, whether thrones or powers or rulers or authorities; all things were created by Him and for Him. He is before all things, and in Him all things hold together.

Colossians 1:15-17

A PRIMARY MOTIVATOR in Olympic competition is the desire of each competitor to be recognized as the best in the world in his event. Eric Heiden, a twenty-one-year-old pre-med student from Madison, Wisconsin, realized that goal in speed-skating as he won all five gold medals in the 1980 Winter Olympics — all in record times! No man had ever won even four winter gold medals and no man had ever swept the speed-skating events. Hundreds of people who couldn't even get into the skating area stood on roof tops and clung to tree limbs to join into the endless chant of "Eric, Eric, Eric!" Eric Heiden left no doubt about who was the "number one" speed-skater in the world.

The apostle Paul had more than skating superiority in mind when he wrote the book of Colossians from a Roman prison around 62 A.D. He wrote to draw attention to the most Supreme Figure in the universe, Jesus Christ. His book should draw our attention and our praise to the Lord Jesus. He is God and He deserves first place over all legalism, philosophy and mystical religion. All Jesus' words smacked of deity, for He alone calmed the sea, fed thousands of people supernaturally, healed the sick and cast out demons. In drawing a word picture of Jesus, Paul lists seven unique characteristics of the Master of the Universe.

First, He is the visible manifestation of the invisible God (v.15) and He radiates God's glory. We, as His children, reflect that glory to others in the world (John 1:18, 14:9).

Second, He is Firstborn of all creation. This means that He preceded all creation and that He is Supreme Sovereign over it. His role in the Trinity is as a Son to the Heavenly Father, with all accompanying rights and privileges.

Third, He is the Creator of all things for His own purpose. This includes a highly organized spirit world as well as the entire material universe. It includes the Milky Way Galaxie, a cluster of stars 10,000 light years wide and 100,000 light years long made up of 100 billion stars (including our own Sun). While it would require 1.2 million Earths and 4.3 million moons to fill a void the size of the Sun, one star, Alpha Centari, is five times larger than the Sun! Jesus created it all and He holds every atom together as well (v. 17). If the Lord Jesus withdrew His hand from His creation for one second all things would disintegrate into oblivion. What a powerful God we have!

Fourth, this glorious Creator is also the leader of His people, all who by faith have trusted Him to save them from their terrible rebellion against the Father. As Head of His body, He will lead us to Heaven!

Fifth, He is the firstborn from the dead. No one else has yet been raised in a glorified body like His. The day is coming when all who are in Christ, whether alive or dead will be glorified with Him (1 Cor. 15). Therefore, He must have preeminence in everything (v. 18)!

Sixth, all the fullness of God dwells permanently in Christ. As a baby in Bethlehem or while hanging on the cross, He was 100 percent God and He could have spoken the universe out of existence at any time. He radiated God's glory; we are to reflect that glory.

Finally,(v.20), He is the Reconciler of all things on earth and in heaven. While things "under the earth" (Phil. 2:10) will one day bow before Him, those doomed there in Hell are not *reconciled* to God. What great peace between repentant man and a Holy God was made by the blood of His cross! This peace means that we who were enemies of God (v.21) become His friends and His children (Eph.2:11-19).

What a wonderful Savior we have! It is impossible for us to be discouraged while we are looking to Him. If we could daily see the real "Number One" as He is in all His power and glory, our outlook would be continually transformed.

QUESTIONS:

1. Who created all things?
2. Why were they created?
3. Who reconciled a Holy God to His rebellious creation?

ACTION POINT:

Fill your mind with thoughts of the Lord Jesus Christ.

Read Colossians 1:24-29

REVELATION OF A MYSTERY

To them God has chosen to make known among the Gentiles the glorious riches of this mystery, which is Christ in you, the hope of glory.

Colossians 1:27

MUCH IRONY AND MYSTERY has often surrounded competition in Olympic events. Consider, for example, the 1500 meters in the 1904 London games. World record-holder Harold Wilson of Great Britain seemed to have victory within his grasp, when Mel Sheppard of the USA began a sprint 100 yards from the finish line. Sheppard passed Wilson and won by a yard and a half! It was the first of four gold medals for Sheppard, who had applied to become a New York policeman and was rejected because officials thought he had a weak heart!

Everyone loves a good mystery and there are several supernatural ones recorded in Scripture. God has revealed to believers (saints) in our age a mystery (a "secret known only by His revelation") which had been hidden for thousands of years. The mystery is that the living Lord Jesus now lives in resurrection power in the lives of both Jews and Gentiles who believe in Him. We are "in Christ" (2 Cor. 5:17, Eph. 1:4) and Christ is "in us" (Rom. 8:10, 2 Cor. 13:5). This is our hope of glory, both now and in Heaven. No wonder we are more than winners! We have a Savior worthy of worship and a hope worth celebrating!

Is Christ living in you? He is if you have agreed with God that you are a sinner, have asked for His merciful forgiveness, and have opened your heart to Him. He makes you an eternal winner, indwelt by the power of the living God. If you have never trusted Him, you are still His enemy, alienated from the power of God because you love sin more than you want Him to rule over you (John 3:19). Like most mysteries, it's hard to comprehend, isn't it? You'll have to accept it by faith.

QUESTIONS:

1. What is a mystery in Scripture?
2. What does it mean to be "in Christ?"
3. How does one get "in Christ?"

ACTION POINT:

Believe what God says about His Son.

Read Colossians 2:1-23

VICTORY
AFTER THE CONFLICT

. . . God made you alive with Christ, He forgave us all our sins, having cancelled the written code, with its regulations, that was against us and that stood opposed to us; He took it away, nailing it to the cross. And having disarmed the powers and authorities, He made a public spectacle of them, triumphing over them by the cross.

Colossians 2:13-15

MANY OLYMPIC COMPETITORS have gone on to further success in other fields after their competitive days. Alfred Gilbert, the pole vaulter who won a 1908 gold medal for the USA, later worked his way through Yale as a magician and eventually became inventor of the Erector Set, an extremely popular toy. Another pole vaulter, Bob Richards (1948-1956), became a minister and a fitness expert. Dennis Weaver (1948 decathlon trials), Johnny Weissmuller (swimming, 1924-1932) and Buster Crabbe (swimming, 1932) all became movie stars. Eric Liddell (400 meters, 1924) became a great missionary. These men and others all enjoyed great victory after the conflict of Olympic competition.

Christians have every reason to enjoy the great spiritual victory after the conflict of the cross of our Lord. That's the reason Paul wrote to the Colossians. He wanted to encourage them and to unite them in love (v.2). In correcting any misunderstanding about Christ, he assured them that all of God was in the omnipotent Jesus (v.9). Observe what Paul says the Lord has done for us:

1. He forgave us all our sins (v.13)! Those who accept His sacrifice on their behalf have been forgiven of past, present and future sins — for all your sins were *future* when He died for you! We need never worry about paying God for our sins, for Christ provided the payment!

87

2. He canceled the written code of rules and regulations that stood against us (v.14). The Law of God had condemned all to death because no one could keep it (Rom. 3:19-20). But Christ took the "death certificate" and marked it "paid in full." He canceled the law by fulfilling it, providing salvation and freedom to all who put their trust in Him!

3. Finally, Jesus completely "disarmed Satan and all his cohorts, exposing publicly the futility of the evil one (v.15). In the old times, captives were often stripped naked as a symbol of defeat and judgment. That is the word used here for what Jesus did to Satan. He made the devil a public spectacle. In Christ we have complete victory over the enemy of our souls and we need never to yield to his enticements to sin! No wonder we are *more than winners* after the competition!

We are not under human traditions or prohibitions. Therefore, we should not submit to legalistic rules made up by men as a measure of spirituality (v. 20-23). Regulations sound spiritual, but lack value in restraining the evil nature and are not to be enforced upon others. The Christian is to be led by God's Spirit in those areas where Scripture is silent. Following man-made rules instead of the still, small voice of the Holy Spirit delays spiritual maturity.

Victory after the conflict is not only possible, it is commanded. We must walk in a way which reflects our position as children of the living God. When this occurs, God is glorified and the world sees the Savior in all of His power!

QUESTIONS:
1. Why can you be considered a winner?
2. What does prevent you from living like a winner?
3. Who is our authority in everything that we do?

ACTION POINT:

Praise God for victory in Jesus by the way you live.

Read Colossians 3:1-18

THE INTERNAL UMPIRE

Let the peace of Christ rule in your hearts, since as members of one body you were called to peace. And be thankful.
Colossians 3:15

THERE ARE MANY DECISIONS in athletics that are difficult to call for the umpires who officiate the race, match, or game. One of them involved the 400M individual medley swimming final during the 1972 Munich summer games. Gunnar Larson of Sweden won the race when he finished only .002 of a second ahead of America's Tim McKee. The margin was less than one-eighth of an inch — about three weeks of growth of one fingernail! The race was so close that sophisticated timing devices had to be used to identify the winner!

When we have to make difficult decisions which trouble mind and soul, we too need help from a "timing device." Certainly we have the Word of God, which sheds light on many matters. But some things are not directly addressed in the Bible. Who to marry, where to live, what job to take, and which meetings to attend are questions that we all have to answer. When faced with decisions like these, Christians have an internal umpire to give them direction. We must let the peace of Christ "act as umpire" in our hearts. In other words, if our affections and our minds are set upon Him (v. 1-2) and God has remade our life style (v.7), a God-given inner tranquility will arbitrate in both interpersonal relationships and in decision-making. When all known sin is confessed, God's peace will calm our minds and we will be void of offense toward others and free to think and decide clearly. In this way, He leads us to make right decisions!

Just as some races must be called with sensitive timing equipment, some decisions must be made with a sensitive spirit to the peace of God. When there's no verse to direct your decision there is always this verse (v.15) pointing to the peace of God. Let His peace guide you in everything — and don't forget to thank Him!

89

QUESTIONS:

1. What are our hearts and minds to be set upon?
2. What kinds of decisions has God clearly spelled out for us in Scripture?
3. What kinds of decisions require special sensitivity to the peace of God?

ACTION POINT:

Seek God for His peaceful direction in a difficult decision.

Read Colossians 3:18-4:1

TAKEOVER
BY HEART AND SPIRIT

Whatever you do, work at it with all your heart as working for the Lord, not for men, since you know that you will receive an inheritance from the Lord as a reward. It is the Lord Christ you are serving.

Colossians 3:23-24

KEE-CHUNG SOHN was a loyal Korean and also a great marathon competitor in the 1936 Berlin Olympics. Because the Japanese were occupying his country, he had to run on the Japanese team in 1936. They even made him change his real name to Kitei Son. In Berlin, he always signed his real name to remind the world that Korea was his real country. Though saddened over the plight of his country, he won the marathon by more than two minutes. In an interview afterward, Sohn commented on his feelings. "The human body can do so much," he said. "Then the heart and spirit must take over."

In Paul's very practical writings to the Colossians, he also writes of the importance of the heart and spirit. We are to become in experience what we already are by position — winners in Christ. That means we must live with a winning attitude regardless of circumstances. It means that there is no distinction between secular and sacred labor, for *all* is to be done as unto God (v.23). In fact, if something cannot be done heartily for God, we ought not do it at all!

As described in Col 3:18-4:1, this principle includes both our home and work life. In the home, wives are to submit joyfully to their husbands. Though not inferior to the man, she is under his authority unless he directs her to act contrary to Scripture. Husbands are to love their wives as they lead them, so they will not be embittered. Children are to cheerfully obey parents, for this pleases God. Fathers must not exasperate children by constant agitation and unreasonable demands. Praise goes much further than criticism of a child. Employees must work hard for employers without keeping an eye on the clock all day. A day's work for a day's pay is pleasing to God and will be rewarded. Employers must be fair and equitable with employees, for employers must answer to God(4:1), Fairness increases the motivation of workers and pleases the Lord.

Has your heart and spirit taken over at home and on the job? As Sohn said, "The human body can do so much." The spirit must take over and motivate each deed in service to the Lord Jesus. Only then is the Father glorified.

QUESTIONS:

1. Why is *how* we work important?
2. Why is *why* we work important?
3. What guideline for decision-making do you see in this principle?

ACTION POINT:

Work with all your heart as though God is your only audience.

Read 1 Thessalonians 4:13-5:11

SMELLING
THE FINISH LINE

For the Lord Himself will come down from heaven, with a loud command, with the voice of the archangel and with the trumpet call of God, and the dead in Christ will rise first.

1 Thessalonians 4:16

GREAT OLYMPIC track competitors have a certain "sixth sense" on the last lap or final stretch of a race. When they sense victory within reach, they begin that extra kick with eyes totally on the goal. It seems that they can almost "smell" the finish line and victory.

In the first letter he wrote in Scripture, Paul emphasizes to the young Christians in Thessalonica that the finish line is imminent. He is saying that the time of God's removal (rapture) of all born-again believers is the next event on the agenda! Though no one knows the date (and we must not try to set it) the stage is set for the return of our Lord for His Church. His return will be announced forcefully and dramatically around the world (4:16). Living believers will join those who have died in Christ to meet the Lord in the air (v.17). His coming will so demonstrate His Lordship that we will meet Him right in the domain of evil spirits (Eph. 2:2, 6:12)!

Paul wrote these words that we might be informed about the future of Christians who have died (v.13), that we might be alert and self-controlled (5:6) and that we might be encouraged (5:11) as we approach the finish line of our earthly existence. Christians should smell victory, for we have much to anticipate! First Corinthians 15:52 says that we will be changed in a flash. The words indicate the smallest division of time, like "the flicker of an eyelid." It will be "show-time" for the glory of our Lord Jesus Christ! By contrast, unbelievers have much to dread, for the catching away of the Church signals the beginning of the wrath of God poured out upon them and there will be no escape (5:3). For those in darkness (moral and spiritual bankruptcy because of rejecting Jesus Christ), There will be a Great Tribulation followed by eternal separation from God.

93

Can you smell the finish line? It is nearer now than ever. The race is not over yet, but when it is over we will win overwhelmingly! That is the message of the glorious gospel of Christ!

QUESTIONS:
1. Why should we not grieve excessively over the death of a Christian?
2. How is Jesus coming to meet his Church?
3. When will He return?

ACTION POINT:

Live in constant expectation of His return.

Read 1 Thessalonians 5:12-28

ATTITUDE CHECK

. . . give thanks in all circumstances, for this is God's will for you in Christ Jesus.

1 Thessalonians 5:18

IN ONLY THE SECOND Olympiad of modern times, Georgetown University's 5'7" Arthur Duffy was the favorite in the 100-meter race. The year was 1900, the site, Paris, and Duffy burst into an early lead. But at the 50-meter mark, he suddenly began to wobble and fall to the ground, the victim of a strained tendon. Later Duffy recalled, "I do not know why my leg gave away. I felt a particular twitching after going twenty yards. I then seemed to lose control of it, and suddenly it gave out, throwing me on my face. But that is one of the fortunes of sport, and I cannot complain."

Arthur Duffy retained an attitude of gratitude in spite of circumstances he did not choose and would not have chosen. Incidentally, in 1902 he ran a 9.6 100-yard dash to set a world record which stood for 24 years. His thankful attitude is a model for us, an example of how Christians should respond at all times.

Paul emphasizes this type of attitude in 2 Thess. 5. Beginning with verse 11, the emphasis of the chapter shifts from our great future hope to our immediate attitudes. Twenty-two commands are given to believers, not to earn or keep our salvation (for that issue was settled by Christ's blood on the cross) but *because* of our salvation. These commands are brief, but vital to victorious living. A scan through the text will reveal the attitudes of believers: "Give thanks in all circumstances, for this is God's will for you in Christ Jesus." We have no right to mope through life. Because God works for our good in everything (Rom. 8:28), we must be thankful in every circumstance. Whether we're rich or poor, healthy or sick, and successful or unsuccessful in this world's eyes, we can be thankful to God in every circumstance. It's a matter of our will — a will to obey God and be thankful.

Take a personal attitude check right now. Are you thankful in everything that is happening? If not, you are

95

disobeying the Lord and probably becoming bitter and cynical. Thank Him for everything (Eph. 5:20) and your whole perspective will change. He will enable you to live as a winner every day.

QUESTIONS:

1. When are Christians to be joyful (v.16)?
2. When are Christians to pray (v.17)?
3. When are Christians to give thanks (v. 18)?

ACTION POINT:

Thank God for the biggest trial in your life.

Read 1 Timothy 4: 1-16

NEVER TOO YOUNG TO WIN

Don't let anyone look down on you because you are young, but set an example for the believers in speech, in life; in love, in faith and in purity.

1 Timothy 4:12

WINNERS IN OLYMPIC contests come from all nationalities, backgrounds, and ages. Many times a young competitor has triumphed over an older one. The youngest Olympic winner in history was Marjorie Gestring of the USA, who won the springboard diving title in the 1936 Olympic games. At the time of her victory, Marjorie's age was 13 years, 9 Months! Yet, she set the standard for much older competitors.

The apostle Paul wrote a letter to a young man, Timothy, encouraging him to also set an example. Because Timothy was younger and may have been somewhat timid and passive, Paul felt a need to continually "spur" him into action as an example for believers. Nothing, not even youth, was to stand in his way and Timothy was not to be intimidated by what others might think of his youthfulness. His speech was to be bold, yet free of pride and arrogance. His life was to be exemplary, a model for all to emulate. By his love and concern for others, Timothy was to draw them to the Lord Jesus. By faith he could stimulate them to trust the Living God. And by purity of thought, work, and deed, the Lord Jesus would be glorified. Moral cleanliness has great influence upon people of all ages.

Today's sports heroes would do well to study the book of 1 Timothy, for all who are given the privilege of athletic stardom also have a responsibility to set good examples for others. Just as Marjorie Gestring became a young Olympic champion, young people can set godly examples for others without being intimidated by what the establishment thinks of their youth. In Christ, no one is ever too young to win!

QUESTIONS:

1. How many young people do you know who are examples to other believers?
2. What type of people do look down on you because of youth?
3. How can you set a godly example to them?

ACTION POINT:

Determine to set an example for others to follow.

Read 1 Timothy 6:3-21

FLEE, FOLLOW, AND FIGHT

But you, man of God, flee from all this, and pursue (follow) righteousness, godliness, faith, love, endurance and gentleness. Fight the good fight of the faith. Take hold of the eternal life to which you were called when you made your good confession in the presence of many witnesses.

1 Timothy 6:11-12

THOUGH SOME CONTESTS had been held around 1100 B.C., the Olympic games were organized in 776 B.C. among the powerful and warlike Greek States. The Greeks, who followed many mythical gods as they made war on one another, agreed to a one-month truce in and around the whole territory of Olympia, site of the ancient games. This gave time for athletes and fans to travel unmolested to and from the games. No man bearing arms, let alone a hostile army, was allowed in the area. This cycle of war and peace, combined with the worship of false gods, was remarkable in a small territory of political and military importance to the world.

As the Greeks would flee violence for a time and follow their gods, Christians are also to *flee* certain things and *follow* the true God, as we fight the good fight of faith. Paul elaborated on these principles in a "leadership manual" to Timothy. He wanted to prepare Christians for the rising tide of opposition that was soon to come. He instructs us to *flee* from false doctrines and the resulting dissention they cause (v.3-5). We are to *flee* from the love of money (v.6-10). We are to *follow* (pursue) such things as righteousness, godliness, faith, love, endurance and gentleness (v.11). Finally, we are to *fight* fiercely the good fight of the faith. In other words, let us give our best effort to hold on to our faith and to spread it to others as the world becomes more and more evil. The "fight" may be inward or outward. It may involve physical suffering as well as spiritual combat. Nevertheless, we must live boldly for Christ ("Take hold of the eternal life to which you were called . . . ." v. 12). He has given us life so that we may live boldly for Him.

99

Do you know what to *flee,* who to *follow,* and when to *fight?* If you were arrested for being a Christian, would there be enough evidence to convict you? Or, like so many people, do you muddle through life in pursuit of money, power and pleasure? It's time for believers to wake up! It's time to win in the "faith fight!"

QUESTIONS:
1. What things are Christians to flee?
2. What traits are Christians to follow?
3. How is the Christian life a fight?

ACTION POINT:

Fight the good fight of the faith.

Read 2 Timothy 1:1-14

OVERCOMING FEAR BY FAITH

For God did not give us a spirit of timidity, but a spirit of power, of love and of self-discipline.

2 Timothy 1:7

SOME ATHLETES have a hard time overcoming a variety of fears as they compete. In the free-rifle competition during the 1912 Olympics, Sergeant Morris Fisher had such a problem. The event required shooting 120 rounds from 300 meters at a 39-inch target with a four-inch bull's eye at the center. Fisher was so nervous, he stood for 20 minutes at the firing line — aiming but not firing! Finally, his coach ordered him to shoot even if he missed the target. He fired a little wide, but then went on to win the match and the gold medal!

Sometimes we live our Christian lives with a tentative, uncertain type of fear. We take our eyes off of the Lord and experience the fear of failure. Some people fear the future and the possibility of suffering. Many even fear success! But the Bible says that this spirit of fear is not from God. He has given us a spirit of boldness to come before Him in prayer, calling Him "Father" and presenting our deepest needs to Him (Rom.8:15). The omnipotent God is our refuge and He supports us in all circumstances (Deut. 33:27).

We need have no fear of opposition to the gospel which we proclaim. We need not be ashamed of God's Word, for it is powerful to save men from sin (Rom. 1:16). The spirit of fear can only come from Satan, who desires to intimidate and discourage Christians. Satan would render us impotent and defeated instead of virile and triumphant in our walk with a loving God. We must not let him do that to us!

Let us trust God and step out by faith, with bold confidence in His might. His spirit of power, love and self-discipline is more then enough to meet all the waves of fear that would threaten our inner peace. As Morris Fisher discovered, once we finally "squeeze the trigger" of our faith, we find the resources to win that we have had all along!

101

QUESTIONS:

1. How does Satan try to rob you of a vital walk with God?
2. What are your greatest fears?
3. How does God enable you to live above fear?

ACTION POINT:

Overcome fear by faith in God.

Read 2 Timothy 2:1-7

COMPETING BY THE RULES

Similarly, if anyone competes as an athlete, he does not receive the victor's crown unless he competes according to the rules.

2 Timothy 2:5

MARATHON RUNNER Frank Shorter of the USA was about to enter the stadium well ahead of the competition during the 1972 Olympics in Munich, Germany. The crowd, especially the American spectators, waited expectantly. Suddenly, an imposter who resembled Shorter appeared through the gate and crossed the finish line. Was he given the gold medal? Certainly not! He had not qualified to run, nor had he run the whole course lawfully.

Between his instruction to serve with the zeal of a soldier (v.4) and to endure as a farmer (v.6), the apostle Paul instructed Timothy to compete as an athlete in his Christian walk. He told Timothy to compete by the rules. Does this mean that we are to live according to a list of laws? No, for Paul has just written that we are to "be strong (passive voice: be empowered or strengthened) in the *grace* that is in Christ Jesus" (v.1). Nevertheless, there are principles we must follow to qualify for the rewards God will one day bestow upon faithful believers. These principles of grace saturate the New Testament. It will take us a lifetime to discover and practice the ways of our Holy God. But let us examine the qualifications for *training* to compete for Christ, for these guidelines resemble those set down for Roman athletes who entered into training.

In ancient Roman days, all competitors had to be free men. No slaves were allowed to compete. Today, all who run the race of faith are free in Christ, for Jesus said, "If the Son shall set you free, you are free indeed" (John 8:36)! Have you been set free by God's Son?

Second, only citizens of the empire who could prove their citizenship were allowed to compete. Likewise, only Christians who are citizens of Heaven and whose lives confirm their citizenship may run the race of faith.

103

Third, an athlete must be morally upright to train. No criminals could compete in the ancient games. Spiritually, God sees believers as clothed in the righteousness of Christ, fully justified before Him! This great fact qualifies the Christian to run the race.

Finally, all competitors must be willing to enter into rigorous training for competition. This meant leaving the comforts of home for at least 10 months to live in a training complex. Similarly, Christians must be willing to leave their sin and to look unto Jesus as the Author and Finisher of their faith. The love of Christ must overshadow the desire for the fleeting pleasures of sin.

Do you qualify for the race God wants you to run? Are you ready to train? Frank Shorter's imposter won nothing because he did not compete according to the rules. Only by training God's way will you and I ever be rewarded before our Heavenly Father for a much more important race!

QUESTIONS:

1. What does it mean to spiritually "enter into training?"
2. How does God see us as believers in Christ?
3. How might God reward believers someday?

ACTION POINT:

Run God's way in the race of life.

Read 2 Timothy 3:10-17

RIGHT INFORMATION ABOUT GOD

All scripture is God-breathed and is useful for teaching, rebuking, correcting and training in righteousness, so that the man of God may be thoroughly equipped for every good work.

2 Timothy 3:16-17

IN 1960, WYM ESSAJAS became the first person chosen to represent the South American nation of Surinam in the Olympics. Unfortunately, he was told that his race, the 800-meters, was to be held in the afternoon. When Essajas arrived at the stadium in Rome, his heats were over and he had to return home without competing! Essajas was given incorrect information and it cost him a chance to compete in the Olympics. It was eight years before the nation of Surinam sent another athlete to the Olympic games.

Wrong information can keep one from learning about and finding our Holy God, for the truth about God is revealed only in His Holy Word. The Bible keeps us safe from the many false teachings in today's world. It was "God-breathed" to the original writers by His inspiration. God used human personalities to record His thoughts, and every word they wrote was ordained by Him (Matt. 5:18). Every word in the original manuscript was written without error ("inerrant") and today's copies are incredibly close to the original text!

God has not only given us His Word, but He has also preserved it throughout all the ages. Even despots like Diocletian have never been able to stamp out the influence of the Bible. This Roman emperor attempted to make Christianity extinct and built a monument on the ashes of what he thought was the last copy of the Scriptures. But 20 years later, another ruler, Constantine, declared Christianity the "state religion," offered a reward for copies of Scripture, and had 50 copies within 48 hours. Others, like the philosopher Voltaire, claimed that within 100 years Christianity would be dead and Bibles would be found only in museums. Yet, 100 years later Voltaire was dead and his

105

own house became the headquarters of the Geneva Bible Society!

In spite of the attacks of liberal theologians who deny the miracles and the inerrancy of the Word of God, the Bible endures forever (1 Pet. 1:24-25). Men who reject God and His revelation do not break down God's Word, but they break *themselves* on His Word. Scripture rebukes us and convicts us of sin so that we may confess and become right with God, then it sets us on a straight path by training us in what is right. Without the Bible, we'd have no God-given standards, no knowledge of God or His will for us. Everyone would just go his own way, doing whatever he deemed "right" in his own eyes. The world would be in chaos without God's word.

How much time do you spend in the Bible each day? Our Father has much to show you if you will read His Word. Better to miss an Olympic race than to miss out on knowing God because of misinformation about Him! Be encouraged, however, the right information is available in His Word.

QUESTIONS:
1. Where does confusion about God originate?
2. Why do many people hate the Bible?
3. What is miraculous about God's Word?

ACTION POINT:

Study God's Word to really know Him.

Read 2 Timothy 4:1-8

RUN TO FINISH

I have fought the good fight, I have finished the race, I have kept the faith.

2 Timothy 4:7

SPRINTER HASELY CRAWFORD, a 6'3" gear machinist from Trinidad, competed in several Olympic events during the 1970s. In Montreal's 1976 games, Hasely suffered a cramp after 50 meters of the 200-meter race and fell to the ground. The official report lists him as not finishing, but a track buff who was watching noted that he never actually left his lane until *after* he had jogged past the finish line. Though his time was rather unusual, he *did* finish the race.

The desire to finish what one starts is an admirable trait sorely lacking in many people of our society. Some people today simply quit when the going gets tough. But always finishing what one starts is the mark of a winner in Christ! A true finisher will complete that half-read book, finish the school term on a positive note, and give his total effort through the last game of the season. God has laid out a course for each of his children to run. As Paul wrote his last letter (2 Timothy) he was in a Roman prison awaiting execution for preaching the gospel. He, like Jesus, could say that he had finished the race that God had laid out for him.

Though the course set for each believer is different, several common features are evident, too. All believers who live godly lives will suffer some sort of persecution (3:12). Each Christian's race is not a sprint, but a marathon. Therefore, running with endurance at a steady pace is vital. Our eyes must be on the Lord Jesus as we run. We must not focus on others or on obstacles. Finally, it is helpful to run with other believers for the mutual encouragement within the group. We need to learn to run together because fatigue seems to creep in more rapidly when running alone.

How are you running the race set before you? Will you cross the finish line with rejoicing when life is over? Let us run a strong race to the finish, looking unto Jesus and the crowns that He will award to us one day!

QUESTIONS:

1. What course has God set before you?
2. How is your course more like a marathon than a sprint?
3. Who must be your focal point as you run?

ACTION POINT:

Run your race to the finish.

Read Hebrews 9:23-10:18

ONCE FOR ALL-TIME

But when this priest had offered for all time one sacrifice for sins, He sat down at the right hand of God.

Hebrews 10:12

WORLD-CLASS ATHLETES know the value of repetition in training for their events. It is only by repeatedly going over the same skill or running the same distances that improvement is made. Such is the purpose of interval training, a method of conditioning which prescribes running a certain distance, followed by jogging or walking a specified distance and then repeating the running distance. This goes on continually until the athlete's capacity for intense exertion is increased to the point where he is fit to compete on a high level!

When it comes to the sacrifice that pays for the sin of man, however, repetition is no longer important! The Bible says that the Lord Jesus appeared once for all time to die for our sins (9:26). While the prescribed Old Testament sacrifices of bulls, goats, pigeons, lambs and other animals were important "types" or examples of the Messiah who was to come, they could never take away sin (10:4). At best, all they could do was "cover" (hide from view) sins (Psalm 32:1; 85:2).

Christ ("the Messiah") came at just the right time and offered one sacrifice for all sins, for all men, for all time! Then our Great High Priest sat down at the Father's right hand (10:12-13). The Old Testament priests never were permitted to "sit down on the job," because their work was never done (10:11). Their sacrifices only reminded people to look forward to the day when the Messiah would come! Just as we look back 2000 years and place our faith in what Christ did for us on the cross, they looked forward by faith to that same "once for all time" sacrifice of the Lord Jesus Christ!

Therefore, there is nothing more we can do for our sin problem! No work, no ritual and no sacrifice is necessary, for He said, "It is finished" (John 19:30). Anything we might try to do would be an insult to a Holy God who paid the full penalty for us! Unlike interval training, repetition is

109

unnecessary. Let us simply agree with God that we are sinners and rest in His forgiveness.

QUESTIONS:
1. What was the purpose of the Old Testament sacrifices?
2. Why are man's works, rituals or sacrifices for sin an insult to God?
3. For how long is Christ's sacrifice for sin valid?

ACTION POINT:

Rest in the finished work of Christ as payment for your sins.

Read Hebrews 10:19-39

ISOLATED
AT THE GOAL LINE

And let us consider how we may spur one another on toward love and good deeds. Let us not give up meeting together, as some are in the habit of doing, but let us encourage one another ---and all the more as you see the Day approaching.
Hebrews 10: 24-25

ONE TACTIC of an offensive-minded soccer team is to isolate a key member of the opposition. Whether it's an Olympic soccer match or a pick-up game, the attacking dribbler tries to get the goalie isolated one-on-one with himself. He then has an excellent chance to score.

Satan tries a similar attack on God's people. If he can get the Christian separated from the encouragement of fellow believers who dynamically love and serve Christ, the Christian is weakened. In his own strength and without encouragement from believing teammates, the Christian often falls into temptation. Everyone needs encouragement. First, we need to give it to those experiencing difficulty in the battle against sin. We must serve such people with comfort, counsel, and prayer. One way of building others in Christ is by teaching a Sunday School class or singing in the choir. Secondly, we need to receive encouragement from Christian friends. Satan tempts us to feel alone in the battle if we let ourselves become isolated from other believers.

Though it is true that some meetings do more harm than good (1 Cor. 11:17-22), there are many churches where God is working in spirit and in truth. It is our responsibility to find a place where Christ is honored and His Word is believed and taught. A close circle of Christian friends upholding one another in prayer is an unbeatable combination. The results are lives lived to the glory of God.

Have you experienced the encouragement that comes from fellowship with other believers this week? If not, the devil has probably isolated you at the "goal line" of glorifying God! Seek out fellowship until you find it. A consistent performance for God requires that you stay close to your teammates.

111

QUESTIONS:

1. Why should Christians meet together?
2. What can be accomplished at God's "team meetings?"
3. What should motivate us to encourage others?

ACTION POINT:

Don't neglect assembling with people who love God.

Read Hebrews 11:1-40

THE HALL OF FAITH

Now faith is being sure of what we hope for and certain of what we do not see.

Hebrews 11:1

AS THE ROMAN EMPIRE deteriorated, more and more blood was shed in gladiatorial combat and in the horrible killing of Christians. The Colosseum had a capacity for housing some 2000 wild beasts of prey for such slaughter. Gladiators entered the arena through the "Door of the Living." "Hail to thee O Caesar; those about to die greet thee" was heard a thousand times in front of the Emperor's box. For 200 years after the apostles, the blood-thirsty masses thrived on the carnage.

In 1300 A.D., a cross was erected in memory of the martyred Christians. It was lost, but in 1927 the Italian government ordered another erected with these words on its base: "Hail to thee, O cross, the only hope!" At the site of pagan rites and rituals, a simple cross reminds the world of the victory of the persecuted. Whether delivered in this life or not, God's people overwhelmingly conquered by faith, assured of what they could not see.

Christians live by that same faith today, whether persecuted physically, socially, or in any other way. We have a tremendous heritage of faithful ancestors. There were Old Testament heroes like Abel, who worshiped God by faith; Enoch, who walked daily with God by faith; Noah, who built the ark by faith; Abraham, who though incredibly rich, lived by faith that God had a better and more permanent home in heaven for him; Jacob, who was a schemer for most of his life and yet is remembered by God as one who worshiped by faith; Joseph, who exercised faith in God's promise to deliver a whole nation from slavery; Moses, who was used by God to deliver Israel because he chose by faith to be mistreated rather than to enjoy the pleasures of sin; the Israelites, who walked through the parted waters of the Red Sea by faith; and Rahab, a prostitute who was in such awe of God that she chose by faith to help His people. Many more experienced overwhelming triumphs by faith. Yet *others*

113

(v.35) exercised faith and suffered apparent defeat. They were tortured and martyred, looking to God by faith for their final and eternal reward in Heaven! Whether in victory or defeat from the world's viewpoint, they were *more than winners* because they lived by faith in the Lord Jesus Christ!

Faith is *obtained* by hearing God's Word (Rom. 10:17) and it is *revealed* by adversity. Whether experiencing victory or defeat in the world's eyes, are you living a life of faith in the Lord Jesus? If so, you are continuing the heritage passed on to you by other members of God's "Hall of Faith."

QUESTIONS:
1. How does God's "Hall of Faith" strengthen you?
2. How do you obtain faith?
3. What gives you the opportunity to demonstrate faith?

ACTION POINT:

Live by faith in God and His Word.

Read Hebrews 12:1-3

EYES ON THE GOAL

Therefore, since we are surrounded by such a great crowd of witnesses, let us throw off everything that hinders and the sin that so easily entangles, and let us run with perseverance the race marked out for us. Let us fix our eyes on Jesus, the author and perfecter of our faith, who for the joy set before Him endured the cross.

Hebrews 12:1-2

FROM THE VERY BEGINNING gymnastics flourished among the Greeks. Young competitors were required to undergo 10 months of training in large areas called "gymnasia." These were large, open-air complexes surrounded by colonnades and rooms where the athletes lived. The competitors were naked and rubbed down only with oil, hence the name "gymnasia" (Gk. gumnos: naked)!

Workouts were held rain or shine. The same basic exercises were done by both runners and wrestlers. All were on a strict diet of meat, dried wheat, fish, cheese, figs and water. No cola and candy bars for these athletes! The demands were strenuous, yet the athletes did not dwell on the agony of training, but on the goal and the victories that were to be won.

The life of a Christian closely parallels the training of a Greek athlete. With respect for the great crowd of witnesses in the stands — men and women who gave their all for Christ — we must get rid of any external hindrance (weights) that restrains us in the contest. Anything that lessens our sensitivity to God must go, whether sinful in itself or not! We must compete whether it rains or shines, bringing glory to our King in all circumstances. All believers undergo the same exercises of prayer, Bible study, and interaction with other believers. Our diet must be the meat of the Word of God and not the world's junk food of off color jokes, television sitcoms, suggestive literature, or pornographic movies. Where do we find the endurance for such training? By fixing our eyes upon Jesus! As His eyes were on the joy set before (Gk. Prokeimenos: the trophies on display at the scorer's table) Him, we must fix our gaze upon our wonderful Lord. We cannot focus upon either the training process or the circumstances. The trophies to be presented one day will be well worth the effort!

QUESTIONS:
1. Who do you think is in the "cloud of witnesses?"
2. What weights keep you from better serving Christ?
3. What was the "joy set before" Jesus?

ACTION POINT:

Keep your eyes on the Lord Jesus.

Read Hebrews 12:4-13

THE DISCIPLINE
OF TRAINING

The Lord disciplines those He loves, and He punishes everyone He accepts as a son.

Hebrews 12:6

A TWENTY-THREE-YEAR-OLD lightweight wrestler from Waterloo, Iowa, endured one of the most disciplined workout schedules possible in preparation for the 1972 Olympics in Munich. Dan Gable trained for seven hours a day, every day for three years prior to the big event. His agony was rewarded when he won the Olympic gold medal! In fact, Dan grew accustomed to reaping rewards for his disciplined lifestyle, as he lost only one match in his entire career!

American Christians could learn much from Dan Gable's disciplined training. Often we fall far short of the disciplined maturity desired by God. But we can thank our Heavenly Father that He disciplines us! In fact, every born-again child of God undergoes the same discipline ("child training")! His discipline of us proves that He loves us and that we are really His children (v.8). Though we sometimes receive punishment for our sins, this is a training form of discipline used by God. He knows just the type of discipline we need! He can send any form of adversity that will build our characters with the kind of strength He desires.

How do you respond to God's discipline? Some people despise it (v.5), "blowing it off" with the fatalistic idea that "since everyone has troubles in life so do I." Others "faint" (v.5), complaining, "Why is this happening to me?" Others stoically endure with the idea that they can "tough it out." But God's idea is that we be trained by adversity (v.11). In other words, we accept trials, thank God for them, and grow stronger, deeper, and closer to Him through them! Only via this reaction will we reap the fruit of God's training.

Dan Gable did not discipline himself for the fun of it. He did it so that he might grow stronger and better prepared for Olympic competition. God disciplines us for a higher

117

purpose. Let His training produce the same results in you through dependence upon Him.

QUESTIONS:
1. What is the difference between "child training" and "punishment?"
2. How has God disciplined you?
3. What does God's discipline prove?

ACTION POINT:

Allow God's discipline to train you.

Read Hebrews 13:1-25

CONTENTMENT
AND A NO-CUT CONTRACT

Keep your lives free from the love of money and be content with what you have, because God has said, "Never will I leave you; never will I forsake you."

Hebrews 13:5

UPON CONCLUDING amateur competition, many of today's superstars obtain contracts worth millions of dollars. Yet, it seems that they are not always satisfied with their agreements. After a good year, some pressure management to "renegotiate" a previous contract for more money. It has gotten to the point that one wonders whether contracts signed by some players are valid!

As Christians, God has commanded us to keep our lives free from greed and to be content with what He has given us. To be constantly grabbing for money is not a Godly characteristic. Furthermore, God has given us reason to be content, for He promises "never to leave or forsake us"(v.5)! This reference, very strongly written in the original text, promises that it is impossible for God to ever leave the Christian. A person who has repented of his sin and trusted Christ may temporarily stumble in ignorance or rebellion against his Heavenly Father, but the Father never lets him go. Two other references (John 6:37-39 and John 10:27-29) are equally emphatic. It is clear that when our Heavenly Father starts conforming us to the image of Christ at salvation, He finishes the job (Rom. 8:29, Phil. 1:6). Therefore, anyone who has come to God by faith alone and trusted nothing but the shed blood of Christ to save Him need never fear losing the precious gift of eternal life!

Why does it seem so many church-attenders "fall away?" Most have never really trusted Christ for salvation in the first place (1 John 2:19). Many place faith in a church, their own works, or baptism to save them. This kind of faith won't save them! Salvation is accomplished by God and is not something man does. A saved person comes to Christ realizing he is morally bankrupt before a Holy God. He casts himself totally upon the mercy and grace of God, trusting in the blood of Jesus. That is salvation. Such a person is sealed by the Spirit of God unto the day of redemption (Eph. 4:30). He still may sin, but his desire is now to please God. He is disciplined by the Father for persistent sin (Heb. 12:5-11).

The question is not, "Will God ever cut me from His team?" Christians have a "no-cut" contract! The question that should be asked is, "Have I trusted Christ alone for salvation in the first place?", "Am I content with the contract He provides by His grace?" or, "Am I really trusting my own works to earn and keep salvation?" You'll never grow up in Him until you rest in His finished work.

QUESTIONS:
1. Who saves us and who keeps us saved?
2. Why would some people not believe they are secure in Christ?
3. Why is it important to know your future is secured?

ACTION POINT:

Rest in the shed blood of Christ for your eternal salvation.

Read James 1:1-18

THE MARATHON OF LIFE

Blessed is the man who perseveres under trial, because when he has stood the test, he will receive the crown of life that God has promised to those who love Him.

James 1:12

THE LONGEST RACE of the Olympics, the Marathon, is named after an ancient Greek city of the same name. The distance of the race is exactly the same as the distance from Marathon to the Greek capital of Athens — 26 miles, 385 yards. The event commemorates the Greek legend of a soldier/runner named Pheidippides, who ran from Marathon to Athens bringing news of the Greek army's victory over the invading Persians in 490 B.C. After his long run he announced "Rejoice, we conquer," and promptly fell dead on the spot!

Pheidippides' long run pictures the course of our lives upon this earth. It is filled with obstacles and must be faced with persistence and patience. James, the half-brother of Jesus, wrote that Christians must face trials with pure joy. We must face trials not with "half-joy" and "half-grief" but with constant rejoicing! These tests of our stamina, when rightly accepted, produce the quality of endurance that God wants to develop in us.

How can we accept trials? Only by faith that God is sovereignly working for our good in them. What good goal does God have for us? He wants us to prove to ourselves and to others that our faith is genuine. He desires our maturity (v.4), our conformity to the image of Christ (Rom.8:29). He wants us to love our Lord Jesus even more and to joyfully anticipate the day we will be with Him in Heaven where there is no suffering! Trials help us towards these goals by "crowding us to Christ." We can accept God's plan by the wisdom He provides for the asking (v.5). He will surely give us all the insight we need when we ask by faith.

The Christian life is not a sprint. It is more like a marathon race. While victory in Heaven is secure, paid for by the blood of the Savior, God wants us to experience victory

121

and maturity here and now. He helps us by sending trials to develop us! As J. Ronald Blue writes,

> To have the right attitude in trials, we must see the advantage of trials, but if it is difficult to see the advantages, one can ask for aid and, if one asks correctly, God will give him the right attitude in trials. He can rejoice in trials and be blessed (v.12) by enduring them. Trials from without and temptations from within are no match for a Christian who stands in the truth from above!

QUESTIONS:
1. What trials have brought you closer to Christ?
2. How must we handle various trials?
3. What power enables us to rejoice in trials?

ACTION POINT:

Thank God as you go through the trials of life.

Read James 3:1-12

MURDER WITH A SMALL, DEADLY WEAPON

All kinds of animals, birds, reptiles and creatures of the sea are being tamed and have been tamed by man, but no man can tame the tongue. It is a restless evil, full of deadly poison.

James 3: 7-8

THE AMERICAN PRESS had boasted that the gold medal in the high jump at Rome's 1960 Olympics was certain to be won by the USA. Joe Faust, Charley Dumas, and John Thomas gave the Americans a great chance to win it all. But Thomas, a mild-mannered teenager who held the world record at 7'3 3/4", was left to fight off three great Russian jumpers alone when Faust and Dumas were hampered by injuries. He finished third, as Robert Shavlakadze of the USSR enjoyed the greatest day of his career and won the gold. Disappointed, yet proud of his third place medal, John Thomas was shocked at the American fans and sportswriters. The same people who had earlier sung his praises turned on him and accused him of getting carried away with the publicity they *themselves* had spread!

The public response left Thomas sick at heart when he realized that people only liked winners. He suffered nightmares for months. Finally accepting that fans are fickle, he decided that American spectators must be frustrated athletes. He concluded, "In the champion, they see what they'd like to be. In the loser, they see what they actually are, and they treat him with scorn."

The little book of James describes the inconsistent words and deeds of people as John Thomas experienced them. What people are made of inside is soon manifested by a small, deadly weapon called the tongue. James describes the tongue as a deadly fire, a word of evil untamable by man. This tremendous power for evil comes straight from hell itself. Like fire, while under control, the tongue can greatly bless others. But out of control, the tongue can devastate like a blaze in a forest. The tongue is the most

123

dangerous weapon in the world, more dangerous than a nuclear bomb.

"On site" inspection of our own words is necessary at all times by all believers! Indeed, control of the tongue is a measure of ones' faith in God (James 1:26). Each of the 30,000 words spoken each day by the average person is heard by God. They are all recorded, and one day men will account for every one (Matt. 12:36-37)! Christians and non-Christians have caused people like John Thomas and others great suffering by their fickle tongues. No believer ought to be guilty of such gossip and slander. Next time you are tempted to gossip, remember that what you say about your neighbor tells more about yourself than it tells about the neighbor! One unknown author has written:

> If your lips would keep from slips
> Five things observe with care;
> To whom you speak, of whom you speak,
> and how, and when, and where.

You are the master of all unspoken words, but once spoken they are the master of you! Only the control of God's Spirit can harness the tongue of any man. woman, or child. Let's be sensitized by Him in everything we say.

QUESTIONS:
1. How is the tongue like a fire?
2. Why can't man tame the tongue?
3. What do your words measure in your life?

ACTION POINT:

Remember that God records each word you speak about others.

Read James 4:13-17

MAN'S PLANS AND GOD'S SOVEREIGNTY

Instead, you ought to say, "If it is the Lord's will, we will live and do this or that."

James 4:15

MOST ATHLETES plan in detail the events they will enter and the training program they will follow. Certainly most plan to win each event they enter, as they well should. But presumptuously planning without considering the sovereign hand of Almighty God is foolish. The experience of hurdler Boyd Gittins underscores the fact that our plans can be changed for us on short notice by events over which we have no control. While competing in the 400-meter hurdle semifinals for the 1968 USA team, Boyd was eliminated when a pigeon dropping hit him in the eye and dislodged his contact lens just before the first hurdle! Though he won a runoff and made the team, a leg injury forced him to withdraw from the first-round heat.

Christians are to plan their courses wisely and even in detail throughout this life. A wise quote says, "He who fails to plan, plans to fail." We need goals toward which to strive. They serve as measuring rods in evaluating where we are and where we are going. We must set dates, times, places, and events so that life proceeds in orderly fashion and achievement is possible. God commends planning and organization and He says we are to plan what is good (Prov. 14:22). But when making our schedules, goals and objectives we must remember that He is sovereign. This means He has the last word (Prov. 19:21)!

God opposes self-sufficient presumption on our part. He has ways of humbling those who boast in their own plans while not considering His will. We are not self-sufficient, for we all need God. Our lives are only a mist that vanishes(v.14) and no man among us knows or controls the future.

So, let us make plans with an awareness of the sovereignty and goodness of God. If we acknowledge Him in everything, He promises to direct our paths (Prov. 3:6). If we

commit our plan to Him, He promises success in the areas
that are important for His purposes (Prov. 16:3-4).

QUESTIONS:

1. Why is it important to plan ahead?
2. What qualifications should we make with every
   goal we set?
3. Who is in ultimate control of a believer's life and
   achievements?

ACTION POINT:

Plan each day with trust in the Sovereignty of God.

Read 1 Peter 2:4-12

DESTINED TO WIN

But you are a chosen people, a royal priesthood, a holy nation, a people belonging to God, that you may declare the praises of Him who called you out of darkness into His wonderful light.

1 Peter 2:9

THE UNEXPECTED AMERICAN ice hockey victory in the 1980 Winter Olympics was a stunning success by a patchwork team. While the sport was dominated by the powerful Russians, the American people were in the midst of an "identity crisis" as world events (Iran, Afghanistan, and inflation) turned against us. Fanatic USA coach Herb Brooks declared to his young team, "Gentlemen, you don't have enough talent to win on talent alone." But equally significant, on the morning of the day when the Americans were to face the best hockey team (amateur or pro) in the world, Brooks inspired the team by declaring, "You're born to be a player. You're meant to be here. This moment is yours. You're meant to be here at this time." This sense of destiny provided the motivation for a frenzied 4-3 upset of the Russians! A final victory over Finland gave America only it's second gold medal in Olympic ice hockey!

Believers in Jesus Christ have an even more exciting destiny to motivate them to Christlikeness. We are chosen by the Lord Jesus, the "Living Stone" rejected by men but precious to God. Because men refuse to humble themselves and trust Him for salvation, they stumble and fall over the Rock (v.8). But we who believe in Him are like "living stones (v.5)", who are part of a great spiritual house of the Lord Jesus, our Chief Cornerstone (v.6). Therefore, we are a "chosen people," greatly prized by God. We didn't choose Him, but He chose us (John 15:16)! We are a "royal priesthood." Every believer is a priest who can personally come into God's presence because of what Christ has done. We need no human priest, for God hears all our prayers (3:12)! We are a "holy nation," purchased by the precious blood of Christ, given by God to Him (John 17:6) and to be revealed when He returns! Though strangers and aliens to

127

this world (v.11), we are destined for the throne . WE ARE DESTINED TO WIN!

Because of who He has made us, our lives should now be different. We have more motivation for performance than the American ice hockey team! We are to declare His praises (v.9) by staying away from sin and living holy lives, for one day even the enemies of Christ will be forced to recognize His Glory!

QUESTIONS:
1. What is the destiny of a believer?
2. What is the believer's relationship to this world?
3. How does your destiny motivate you?

ACTION POINT:

Let your performance match your destiny.

Read 1 Peter 4:12-19

THE PRESSURE
AND THE PURPOSE

Dear friends, do not be surprised at the painful trial you are suffering, as though something strange were happening to you.

1 Peter 4:12

VERA NIKOLIC of Yugoslavia felt extreme pressure during the 1968 Olympics at Mexico City. The twenty-year-old favorite, a world-record holder in the 800-meters, was her nation's only hope of a medal. She became so distraught that after 300 meters she dropped out and left the stadium. Rumors spread that she had gone to a nearby bridge and was prevented from committing suicide by her coach who had followed behind her.

When Peter wrote his first letter, Christians were feeling even more extreme pressure than Nikolic! A great persecution under Nero was spreading throughout the empire. Christians had been blamed for the burning of Rome. Some were covered with pitch and used as living torches to light the Imperial gardens at night. Therefore, Peter's words about pressure and suffering were desperately needed and accepted. He wrote that we should not be surprised when we suffer, but we should accept it joyfully. Suffering is not accidental for a believer, but is normal Christian experience (1 Cor. 10:13). Therefore, we must not ask, "Why me?" when we suffer. After all, "Why not us?" When we suffer, we must remember that God sends trials for our good (Rom. 8:28-29)! Since this is true, it would be sad to be found complaining about trials when Jesus comes! He expects us to get all the benefit possible from each trial we are called upon to endure. That's God's method of conforming us to the image of Christ!

Someone has written, "God never does, nor suffers to be done but what we ourselves would do, could we see the future as well as He." Annie Johnson Flint wrote:

God hath not promised skies always blue,
    Flower-strewn pathways all our lives through;
God hath not promised sun without rain,
    Joy without sorrow, peace without pain.

God hath not promised we shall not know
    Toil and temptation, trouble and woe;
He hath not told us we shall not bear
    Many a burden, many a care.

God hath not promised smooth roads and wide
    Swift, easy travel, needing no guide;
Never a mountain, rocky and steep,
    Never a river, turbid and deep.

But God hath promised strength for the day,
    Rest for the laborer, light for the way,
Grace for the trials, help from above
    Unfailing sympathy, undying love.

Has extreme pressure caused you suffering today? Is it because of a broken relationship with someone? Has a close friend let you down or turned against you because of a misunderstanding that cannot be rectified? Have you encountered a death or a divorce? A severe injury? Are you ostracized for your faith in Christ? If any of these is true, you must be patient. Through Christ you can handle the pressure. Suffering identifies you with Him! Commit yourself to a faithful God and keep doing good. He will never fail you.

QUESTIONS:
1. Of what benefit is suffering?
2. Why do Christians sometimes suffer?
3. How should we suffer?

ACTION POINT:

Praise God that suffering identifies you with Jesus.

Read 1 Peter 5:1-11

LION ON A CHAIN

Be self-controlled and alert. Your enemy the devil prowls around like a roaring lion looking for someone to devour. Resist him, standing firm in the faith . . . .

1 Peter 5:8-9

MUNICH, GERMANY, was the host city for the 1972 Olympics, as the West Germans hoped to erase the embarrassment of the 1936 Nazi games. But eight Palestinian terrorists went on the prowl, carrying athletic bags with machine guns and hand grenades into the Olympic village where the Israeli athletes stayed. Two Israelis were killed immediately and nine taken hostage, as the terrorists demanded the release of 200 political prisoners held in Israel. Subsequently, all 11 Israeli athletes, five terrorists, and one policemen were killed in gunfire at the airport. Although the games continued (after a 34-hour suspension and memorial service) many athletes had lost their desire to compete.

Christians have an enemy on the prowl that is even more deadly than a Palestinian terrorist! His name is Satan ("adversary"), and he is engaged constantly in accusing us before the Father in Heaven. Originally created by the Lord Jesus (Colossians 1:16) for the praise and adoration of the Most High, he was a beautiful and holy creature. But one day, iniquity was found in him (Ezekiel 28:15) and God judged him. His chief sin was pride and a self-centered desire to "be like the Most High" (Isaiah 14:13-15). Though not all-powerful, all-knowing, or everywhere present (only God has these attributes), one-third of Heaven's angels followed him! He became the god of this world when Adam also followed him in rebellion against God.

Satan is a personal devil. He capitalizes on our own ignorance of his methods. He is experienced, having at least 7,000 years of practice since Adam and Eve! He knows our weaknesses, our desires, our ambitions and our motives. Because he cannot get at God, Satan has declared total war on God's redeemed children. He attempts to rob God of the glory due Him through His creation. He will do

131

anything to make Christians live as discouraged, depressed and defeated believers. To rob us of peace and joy, he will de-emphasize prayer and the study of God's Word. He will tempt us to feel self-sufficient. His "prowling about" is to tempt us in three basic areas: the lust of the flesh, the lust of the eyes, and the pride of life (1 John 2:16).

Yet, as Martin Luther wrote, Satan is only a "lion on a chain held by an omnipotent God!" If he tries to tempt us beyond our ability to endure, God "yanks him back." The loving Father will only allow him to tempt us within our ability to overcome (1 Cor. 10:13). We are to resist him (James 4:7) when tempted to worry, lust, doubt God, covet, gossip, lie, procrastinate, or become lazy, discontent or selfish.

Like a lion which devoured Christians in the Roman coliseum, Satan would like to destroy us. But thanks to the victory won by Jesus on the cross., we have the authority (and responsibility) to resist him when harassed and tempted. As we trust the Lord Jesus Christ for deliverance from the evil one, Satan must flee and the peace and joy return.

QUESTIONS:
1. How powerful is Satan in comparison to man?
2. How powerful is Satan in comparison to God?
3. What are Satan's most frequent methods in your life?

ACTION POINT:

Resist the devil when he tempts you to sin.

Read 1 John 1:1-10

GET UP AND BREATHE!

If we confess our sins, He is faithful and just and will
forgive us our sins and purify us from all unrighteousness.

1 John 1:9

ITALY'S DORANDO PIETRI was the first of 75 runners to
enter the stadium in London's 1908 Olympic Marathon race.
But he started around the track in the wrong direction and
the cries of spectators alerted him to turn the other way.
Then he collapsed, struggled to his feet, collapsed again, got
up, and fell 3 more times. The chief clerk and a medical
attendant rushed to his side and helped him across the finish
line. But their actions caused Dorando to be disqualified
and an American, 5'4" John Hayes, was declared the
winner!

Our spiritual lives sometimes resemble the constant
falling down of the Italian Marathon runner. We fall down
because of sin, and the only way to get back on our feet is to
confess that sin to God. What is confession? It simply
means to "agree with God that we have sinned." He says that
we fall in thought, word and deed. He knows all the evil
imaginations, intents, and motives of our hearts! When we
were saved by trusting Christ, our positional *union* with
Christ was secured, but as we run the race of life, our
practical *communion* with Him varies. Because of the old
sinful nature which remains with us until death, we need to
keep "getting up off the track" by confessing our sin to the
Father. He is faithful and just, and forgives us of all sin,
even those of which we are unaware (v.9)!

To deny our sin is to be self-deceived. If we try to cover it
up, we fail to deal with sin as God prescribes (v.8). But how
wonderful to confess, receive forgiveness, and be cleansed
of all impure thoughts, motives and evil desires! It's like a
fresh breath of pure country air! Our relationship with God
can be one of harmony and peace because of the continuing
power of the blood of Christ shed on the cross for our
forgiveness!

Next time you "fall down" under the weight of sin, get back
on your feet by agreeing with God that you have sinned. He

133

will put you back in the race. As you "breathe spiritually" through confession of sin and receiving His forgiveness, you will live in His purity and power.

QUESTIONS:

1. What does God say about the person who says he has no sin?
2. What does "confession" mean?
3. What does God do when we confess sin?

ACTION POINT:

Confess all known sins to God and believe Him for forgiveness.

Read 1 John 2:1-17

THE LOVE GOD HATES

Do not love the world or anything in the world. If anyone loves the world, the love of the Father is not in him.

1 John 2:15

DESPITE THE ABSENCE of many of its best amateur players, the 1968 U.S.A. basketball team carried on a tradition of excellence by winning another gold medal in Mexico City. In fact, the Americans concluded the tournament having never lost, a streak that included 54 games and stretched back to 1936 when basketball was added to the Olympics. Led by Spencer Haywood and Jo-Jo White, the Americans ran away from Yugoslavia in the final game, scoring 65-50 victory. The vocal Mexican crowd, which had been rooting for the underdog Yugoslavia team, was so awed by the American athletes that they switched allegiance during the game!

Changing allegiance in a basketball game has not nearly the consequences of changing allegiance in life. It is of great concern to God when a Christian becomes more loyal to the things of this world than he is to the Lord who has saved him. God hates such changes in loyalty and has warned us to "love not" the world. In fact, many people who love this world system are merely *professors* of salvation and not *possessors!*

A Christian committed to living for God will obey Christ's commands (v.3). This does not mean the Ten Commandments given to Israel in the Old Testament. These commandments are a "mirror" to be looked at to reveal that we are sinners and unable to keep the law (Rom. 3:19-26, 5:20, 7:4-25). New Testament commands include such things as found in 1 Thess. 5:16-18: to rejoice always, to pray continually and to give thanks in *all* circumstances. Christ commanded us to love one another (John 15:12) and to go into all the world with the gospel (Matt. 28:18-20). We are also told to bear one another's burdens (Gal. 6:2).

135

A Christian committed to living for God will walk as Jesus walked — in humility and self-sacrifice (v. 6). He will love his brother (v. 10), considering others as better than himself (Phil. 2:3).

A Christian committed to living for God will not love this world. What is the "world?" It does not mean the trees, mountains, and rivers that God created, but it is the sinful system in which we live. This world system is attractively arrayed and organized to function independently of God. The world system of politics, culture, education, business and even religion is a rival to God, for it seeks to leave God out! We can become immersed in the world for days and weeks, involved with its problems and never consider God! We can even sit in church and leave God out of our lives. Our God loves the men of the world (John 3:19), but not the system that organizes them against Himself! To become a friend of that system is to be an enemy of God (James 4:4), for the whole world is under the control of Satan (1 John 5:19). Therefore, all God's children are on enemy territory. As winners in Christ, let us never switch allegiance. We must *use* but never *love* the things of this passing world (1 Cor. 7:31)!

We cannot serve two masters (Matt. 6:24). God and the world are as opposed to each other as light and darkness. What makes them opposed? Verse 16 tells us that the world includes the cravings of man for sensual gratification. Secondly, the world includes the lust of the mind with its greedy longings for esthetic gratification. Thirdly, the world includes the boasting of man's independence of God. All these come from the world, which is passing away. Because of who we are in Christ, let us "fix our eyes upon Jesus" and walk in the light of His truth. In loving God, we will never love the things God hates!

QUESTIONS:
1. What is meant by the "world?"
2. What are some of Christ's commands?
3. What are some evidences that a person is a Christian and committed to living for God?

ACTION POINT:

Love God and not this world system.

Read 1 John 5:1-15

WE GROW
BECAUSE WE KNOW

I write these things to you who believe in the name of the Son of God so that you may know that you have eternal life.
1 John 5:13

WHAT A PERSON doesn't know *can* hurt him in athletics. Seventeen-year-old Bob Mathis (who won the decathlon in 1948), is an example. After putting the shot over 45 feet, he left the throwing circle from the front. An official signaled "foul", and the perplexed Mathis was only able to throw 42 feet 9 1/4 inches thereafter. No one had ever told him the rule that a shot-putter must leave the circle from the rear.

Not knowing where he stands can severely hurt a person in his spiritual life as well. That's why 1 John was written (v.13). We must *know* our position in Christ so that we can grow in our practice of the Christian life. How can we know whether or not we are saved? First, if we have repented of sin and trusted Christ alone for salvation, we will love other believers and will obey God's commands (v.1-3). We have the internal witness of the Holy Spirit which confirms the reality of Christ (v.6-10). Once we have trusted Christ, we can never lose our salvation, for God cannot lie (John 6:37, 10:28, Hebrews 13:5). We were sealed with God's Spirit, which guarantees our inheritance (Eph. 1:13-14). He will finish the work He began in us (Phil. 1:6) in conforming us to the image of Christ (Rom. 8:29).

Knowing we are *secure* in Christ, we can have daily *assurance* in Christian living. We can be bold in prayer (v.14-15) and be always joyful, knowing that our salvation does not depend upon our performance. Because we have no fear of being lost, we need not fall into legalism — trying to do things to appease God. Those who fall into such a trap never grow in grace and are robbed of the joy of Christianity, for grace plus works as a means of salvation can never mix. To mix the two is to destroy the very principle of grace. Any works we do must be a *result* of God's grace in saving and keeping us!

Like the two Olympic decathlon athletes, don't be hurt by what you don't know. Remember, we are saved and kept by God's grace through faith, totally apart from works on our part. Relax and enjoy His salvation and you will grow in Him!

QUESTIONS:
1. What is the basis of salvation?
2. Why is it important to know where you stand?
3. How does our position relate to our performance?

ACTION POINT:

Learn all you can about God's great salvation.

Read Jude 1-23

DECEIVED
BY AN IMPOSTER

. . . contend for the faith that was once for all entrusted to the saints. For certain men whose condemnation was written about long ago have secretly slipped in among you.

Jude 3-4

THOUGH STANISLAWA WALASIEWICZ was born in 1911 in Poland, her family soon moved to Cleveland, Ohio, where she grew up as Stella Walsh. On May 11, 1930, she became the first woman to run 100 yards in 11 seconds. Running for Poland in the 1932 Olympics, she tied three world records. She represented her country again in the 1936 Berlin games.Before concluding her career, Walsh set 11 world records, winning 41 AAU titles and two Olympic medals.

However, her story has an ironic ending. While shopping in Cleveland in December of 1980, she was caught in the crossfire of a robbery attempt and shot to death in a parking lot. An autopsy revealed that Stella had male sexual organs! While winning all those women's races throughout her life, Stella Walsh had in fact been a man!

Stella Walsh has not been the only imposter to deceive the world. There are a great many people posing as ministers of Christ who are deceiving people in an even more important race — the great race of faith! Jude wrote a short letter to Christians warning us to be aware of such deception and to *contend* for the truth which God has given us. Therefore, let us contend without becoming contentious (2 Tim. 2:24-26).

In this day of apostasy, there are ministers who deny practically every basic tenet of Christianity. What are some marks of false teachers who have intruded into the church? They are godless men who are given into immorality and who deny the person and work of Jesus Christ (v.4). They reject authority and slander spiritual powers which they do not comprehend (v.8). They are self-centered and, though standing in the pulpit of churches as preachers, they do not feed the people anything of substance (v.12). They resemble clouds without rain! They grumble in undertones against

139

God because of their lot in life and they find fault with others (v.16). They spend their lives on their own desires for food, fun, and fame and use great flowery words to flatter others and boast about their achievements (v.16).

How can we discern such false teachers? Like treasury agents who become so familiar with real money that counterfeit bills are recognized immediately, we must study God's Word so that we can quickly perceive every deviation from the truth. This is how we are "built up in the faith (v. 20). We must pray in the power of the Holy Spirit (v.10), for even when we are unsure of how to pray, the Spirit makes intercession for us (Rom. 8:26). We must keep ourselves open to the love of God, waiting for the merciful coming of Christ to take us to be with Him (v. 21)!

Don't become discouraged because of imposters in athletics or in churches. The presence of the false implies the reality of the genuine! Let us keep our eyes upon Jesus and we will quickly discern the false from the true.

QUESTIONS:
1. How can you "contend for the faith?"
2. What are some marks of a false teacher?
3. What is your defense against false teaching?

ACTION POINT:

Study God's Word for yourself to avoid being deceived.

Read Jude 17-25

GLORY!

To Him Who is able to keep you from falling and to present you before His glorious presence without fault and with great joy — to the only God our Savior be glory, majesty, power, and authority, through Jesus Christ our Lord, before all ages, now and forevermore! Amen!

Jude 24-25

THERE HAVE BEEN miraculous performances in Olympic competition, from Jesse Owen's victories in the 1936 "Nazi Games" to the 1980 USA hockey triumph. There have been dominating teams in various sports — the USA in basketball and the Russians in ice hockey. There have been dynamic Olympic champions like Jim Thorpe, Emil Zatopek, Bruce Jenner, Nadia Comaneci and Mary Lou Retton. But the glory of no individual or team performance compares to the matchless glory of our God and Savior, Jesus Christ. He deserves glory, praise and honor above and beyond anyone or anything else, now and for all time.

As Jude explodes with highest praise, let all those whom He has redeemed and placed on the "winning team" proclaim how great He is! He is able to keep us from stumbling, despite the pressure from our enemies (world, flesh and devil)! He will present us blameless before the presence of God through His saving and keeping power! Great joy will accompany our appearing in His presence on that day! Paul could hardly contain himself as he wrote of the glory of God:

God, the blessed and only Ruler, the King of Kings and Lord of Lords, Who alone is immortal, and Who lives in unapproachable light, Whom no one has seen or can see. To Him be honor and might forever! Amen.

1 Tim. 6:15-16

He is glorious and glorified! Check the apostle John's description in Revelation 1! He is majestic and powerful! Check the account of all the hosts of heaven in Revelation 19! He is authoritative forever and will make all things new

141

(Revelation 21). He deserves the highest praise and adoration of all creation. Let us bow down and worship before Him!

QUESTIONS:
1. What is worship?
2. Why does God deserve worship?
3. When do you best worship the Lord?

ACTION POINT:

Worship God in spirit and in truth.

Read Revelation 2 and 3

POOR REPRESENTATIVES

So, because you are lukewarm — neither hot nor cold — I am
about to spit you out of my mouth. You say, "I am rich; I have
acquired wealth and do not need a thing." But you do not
realize that you are wretched, pitiful, poor, blind, and naked.
Revelation 3:16-17

IN 1972 AND 1976, Haitian runners consistently finished in
last place in Olympic competition. Though Haiti is a poor
country, the reason for their dismal finish was political.
Instead of holding tryouts for the national team, the dictator
of Haiti, "Baby Doc" Duvalier, chose his friends and most
trusted soldiers to compete! No wonder they represented the
country so poorly. None were very good athletes!

Because our Lord is so concerned about how He is
represented here on earth, He wrote letters to the seven
churches of Asia Minor. These form chapters 2 and 3 of the
book of Revelation. God had a particular rebuke for the
Laodicean church, for it claimed to be something that it
really was not. The letter applies not only to the Laodicean
church but to many churches and individuals today.
Though the city was a place of great wealth, commerce, and
culture, the church had become spiritually indifferent. The
Lord used a local illustration to reveal its pitiful condition.
Ice-cold water was piped from the mountains around
Laodicea to the city. But by the time it reached the city, it was
lukewarm. Hot springs were also found in a nearby valley,
but they too became lukewarm before reaching the city.
Many people drink ice water and others enjoy hot water, but
few, if any, will choose lukewarm water to drink. They just
spit it out.

The same is true for a lukewarm church or individual. To
be hot for the Lord, in love and service, is great. On the other
hand, if one is ice-cold and knows it, he can repent and come
to Christ to meet his needs. But a lukewarm person thinks
that he has no need to repent and get closer to God. Like so
many American churches which are content with beautiful
buildings, material wealth, and elaborate programs, the
lukewarm person lacks the fortitude to stand for truth. He

143

rides the fence on vital issues and compromises his convictions, if he has any convictions at all. This hypocrisy is nauseous to the Lord Jesus! Better be cold toward Christ than a *professing* Christian who doesn't really *possess* Christ personally. Jesus will vomit such churches and individuals out of His mouth (v.16).

What is your condition today? Are you hot, cold or a hypocritical lukewarm — thinking that you have no needs? If you are lukewarm, you are a worse representative of Christ than a Haitian politician who represents his country in the Olympics. Christ knocks on the door of your heart, waiting for you to repent, open the door, and let Him in (Rev. 3:20). He will change you if you will repent.

QUESTIONS:
1. Why is a lukewarm person disgusting?
2. How is the modern church lukewarm?
3. What is the first step to getting out of a lukewarm condition?

ACTION POINT:

Repent of all lukewarmness and become hot for Christ!

144

Read Revelation 20:1-15

THE TRAGEDY OF DELAY

If anyone's name was not found written in the book of life, he was thrown into the lake of fire.

Revelation 20:15

IN 1972, VALERY BORZOV of the Soviet Union was the clear favorite in the 100-meters at Munich. But Eddie Hart and Rey Robinson of the USA. had each run 9.9 in the Olympic trials and were considered contenders. All three won first round heats on the morning of August 31. The second round was scheduled for 4:15. As time drew near, Hart and Robinson didn't show up, and a third American runner went frantically searching for them. Thinking the quarterfinals didn't begin until 7:00, Hart and Robinson were waiting for a stadium bus when they happened to see a TV monitor. They were shocked to see the runners lining up for the 100 meters. Driven at breakneck speed to the stadium, the Americans arrived too late at the stadium and lost their opportunity to compete. Their mistaken delay had turned into tragedy.

There is another kind of delay that results in far greater tragedy than missing one's Olympic event. That is the failure of a person to receive Jesus Christ as personal Savior before physical death, for there awaits such a person only judgment and eternal destruction (2 Thess. 1:9). The Bible is very clear about the consequences of delay in coming to Christ, for Jesus spoke more of Hell than He did about Heaven.

From Revelation 20, we know that a day is coming (after a Great Tribulation of seven years) when Satan will be locked in "the abyss" while Christ reigns for 1000 years on earth. He will then be released and will gather a great army, which God will destroy with fire (v.7-9). Then he will be thrown into a lake of burning fire to suffer forever (v.10). The Judgment of the dead before the great White Throne follows, during which time the "Book of Life" is opened (v.12). All whose names are not written in this book will be thrown into the lake of fire (v.15)! Just as Heaven for the Christian will be a thousand times better than words can describe, Hell will

145

be a thousand times worse for the unsaved. Those who have rejected Christ and Heaven will have the only alternative - Hell and Satan. They will be salted with unquenchable fire (Mark 9:42-49).

It won't be a time to "party with friends," for the Bible describes Hell as a place of weeping and gnashing of teeth (Matt. 13:40-42). Hell is a place of blackest darkness (2 Pet. 2:17) and everlasting destruction apart from God (2 Thess. 1:9). Created for the devil and his angels (Matt. 25:41), man chooses to go there rather than admit his sin and trust Christ for his salvation. Those who refuse Jesus as Savior will have Him as Judge, for the Father has committed all judgment to the Son (John 5:22). Though many escape punishment for crimes in this life, *no one* will escape on that day, for God's written records are totally accurate.

The most vital question of all time is, "Has your name been written in the 'Lamb's Book of Life?'" If not, *do not* wait to admit to God you are a sinner. Ask Him to forgive and save you! Tell another person of the need to repent without delay. The consequences of delay are far too great!

QUESTIONS:

1. What happens to a person who dies without repenting of his sin?
2. Why is a literal Hell a certainty for unbelievers?
3. What is the danger of delay in accepting Christ?

ACTION POINT:

If you have never done so, repent of sin and trust Christ.

Read Revelation 21 and 22

A NEW BEGINNING

He will wipe every tear from their eyes. There will be no more death or mourning or crying or pain, for the old order of things has passed away. He who was seated on the throne said, "I am making everything new!"

Revelation 21:4-5

IN 1907, NEW YORK CITY police officer Dennis Horgan was attacked when he tried to break up a brawl. He was brutally beaten with sticks and shovels and nearly killed. His recovery and subsequent shot put of 44' 8 1/4" in the 1908 London Olympic games was remarkable, especially since he was 37 years old! After his surprising recovery, he was given a pension and allowed to return to Ireland, where he enjoyed a new beginning.

One day, God will change the order of things from time to eternity, giving a new beginning to all who are part of His kingdom. This is the final revelation of God to man, and is recorded in the last two chapters of Revelation. Sin, sorrow, pain, death, and all foes opposed to God are forever put away! God will create a new Heaven and new earth and He will personally dwell with all saved individuals of all time! This includes anyone who will come to Christ now and accept His free gift of the "Water of Life (22:17)!"

Not much is told of the new Heaven and new earth. We do know that we will live in a Holy City, the New Jerusalem, which is totally free from sin and all its effects. Righteousness will reign universally (2 Pet. 3:13)! All the potential we were created to fulfill will be realized! We know that there will be no sun necessary, for the glory of God is bright enough (21:23)! There will be no more sea (21:1), so the entire mass of the planet will be inhabitable.

The entire plan of God in creation will be realized in Heaven's eternal state. God has accomplished His purpose: He now has eternal fellowship with a free moral agent who chooses to worship and serve Him forever! Sin is absent for all time and is not even a memory. The living is "out of this world!" In short, "God Wins" and because we've trusted Christ, "WE WIN!"

147

QUESTIONS:

1. What is the greatest thing about Heaven?
2. How large is the New Jerusalem?
3. Who may come to Christ today?

ACTION POINT:

Joyfully anticipate the fulfillment of Heaven!

Appendix I

The Winning Run

PERHAPS YOU HAVE READ this book, but never personally trusted the Savior with your earthly life and your eternal destiny. The following baseball illustration explains how you can come to know the Lord Jesus Christ:
In baseball, a runner must touch all four bases to score a run for his team. The path to abundant and eternal life is very similar to the base paths on a ball diamond.

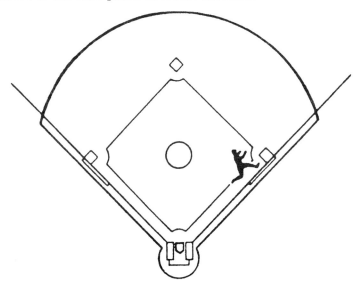

Step 1 (first base) along that path is realizing that God cares about you. He not only created you, but He also loves you very deeply. He is seeking to give you an abundant life now and for eternity.

For God so loved the world that He gave His one and only Son, that whoever believes in Him shall not perish but have eternal life.   John 3:16

I have come that they may have life, and have it to the fullest.
John 10:10

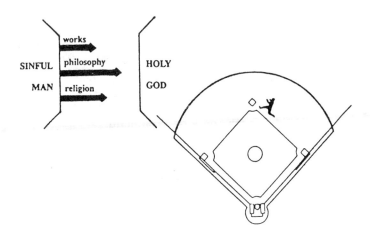

At second base (step 2) we admit that we are sinners and separated from God. He is perfect, pure, and good; we are not. Because by nature we disobey Him and resist Him, He cannot have fellowship with us without denying His goodness and holiness. Instead, He must judge us.

Whoever believes in Him is not condemned; but whoever does not believe stands condemned already, because he has not believed in the name of God's one and only Son.
John 3:18

We realize we can never reach God through our own efforts. They do not solve the problem of our sin.
For all have sinned and come short of the glory of God.
Romans 3:23

But your iniquities have separated you from your God; your sins have hidden His face from you, so that He will not hear.
Isaiah 59:2

For the wages of sin is death, but the gift of God is eternal life in Christ Jesus our Lord.
Romans 6:23

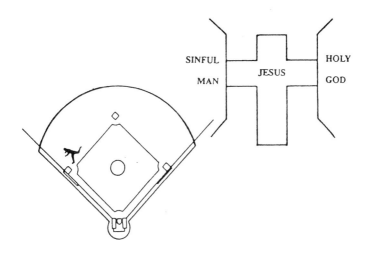

Third base is so close to scoring. Here (step 3) we understand that God has sent His Son, Jesus Christ, to die on the cross in payment for our sins. By His sacrifice, we may advance Home.

But God demonstrates His own love for us in this: While we were still sinners, Christ died for us.

Romans 5:8

For Christ died for sins once for all, the righteous for the unrighteous, to bring you to God.

I Peter 3:18

Jesus answered, "I am the way and the truth and the life. No one comes to the Father except through Me."

John 14:6

However, being CLOSE to Home does NOT count!

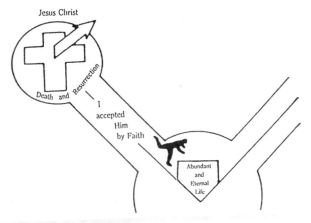

The Winning Run!

To score (step 4), we must personally receive Jesus Christ as Savior and Lord of our lives. We must not only realize that He died to rescue people from their sin but we must also trust Him to rescue us from our own sin. We cannot "squeeze" ourselves home any other way, and He will not force Himself upon us.

Yet to all who received Him, to those who believed in His name, He gave the right to become children of God.

John 1:12

For it is by grace you have been saved, through faith — and this is not from yourselves, it is the gift of God — not by works, so that no one can boast.

Ephesians 2:8-9

Why not receive Jesus Christ as your Savior and Lord right now? Simply say: "Yes, Lord," to His offer to forgive you for your sins and to change you.

(signed) _____

(date) _____

Tell someone of your decision and keep studying God's Word. These things greatly strengthen you (Romans 10:9-10). You may write *The Winning Run Foundation* for further encouragement. We would be thrilled to hear of your commitment! Welcome to eternal life!

Appendix II

The Perfect Reliever

THE FOLLOWING BASEBALL illustration explains how to walk consistently in the power of the Holy Spirit, our only hope for victory in spiritual warfare.

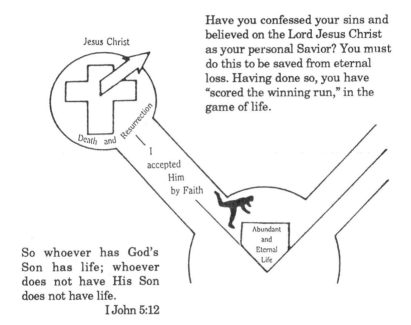

Have you confessed your sins and believed on the Lord Jesus Christ as your personal Savior? You must do this to be saved from eternal loss. Having done so, you have "scored the winning run," in the game of life.

So whoever has God's Son has life; whoever does not have His Son does not have life.
I John 5:12

YOU SIGNED WITH THE WINNING TEAM WHEN YOU RECEIVED CHRIST!

1. Your sins were forgiven (Colossians 1:14)
2. You became a child of God (John 1:12)
3. God in dwelt you with His Spirit so you may live victoriously over the world (John 15:18-19), the flesh (Romans 7:15-18), and the devil (I Peter 5:8).
4. You began the process of discovering God's purpose for your life (Romans 8:29).

BUT.... WHAT'S HAPPENING NOW?

Though our Lord has assured all His children of eternal life (John 10:28) and our position in Christ never changes, our practice may sometimes bring dishonor to God. The enemy rally makes life miserable.

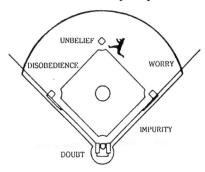

The enemy's dugout:
- Prayerlessness
- No desire for Bible Study
- Loss of love
- Legalistic attitude
- Jealousy
- Guilt

This rally must be stopped, for the Bible makes it clear that no one who belongs to God can continually practice sin (I John 2:3; 3:6-10).

These two pitchers' mounds represent the two lifestyles from which a Christian must choose:

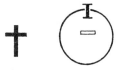

Self in control of the game and Christ's Resurrection power waiting in the bullpen — enemy rally produces discord.

Power of Christ replaces self on the mound — rally is stopped and peace is restored.

For we naturally love to do evil things that are just the opposite from the things that the Holy Spirit tells us to do.

...and the good things we want to do when the Spirit has His way with us are just the opposite of our natural desires. Galatians 5:17a)

SO WHAT'S THE SOLUTION?

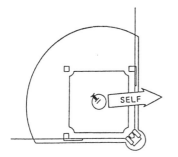

BRING IN THE PERFECT RELIEVER!

We must step off the mound and allow God to have complete authority by giving control of the game to the Holy Spirit.

Only by giving the Holy Spirit of God His rightful place of authority over our every thought, word and deed, can we consistently overcome defeat and despair.

If we are living now by the Holy Spirit's power, let us follow the Holy Spirit's leading in every part of our lives.

Galatians 5:25

WHAT DOES THE HOLY SPIRIT DO?

When you received Jesus Christ as Savior, the Holy Spirit indwelt you (Romans 8:9). Though all who have received Christ are indwelt by the Spirit, not all are filled (empowered, motivated) by the Spirit.

The Holy Spirit:

a. Instructs us in all things.
b. Always glorifies Jesus Christ (John 25:26; 16:13-15).
c. Convicts us when things are wrong in our lives. (John 16:7-8).
d. Helps us to share Christ with others (Acts 1:8).
e. Assures us we belong to Christ (Romans 8:26).
f. Enables us to live above circumstances through prayer (Romans 8:26).
g. Flows from us as the source of an abundant and victorious life. (John 7:37-39).

HOW CAN YOU BE FILLED?

You can be filled (motivated) by the Holy Spirit right now IF YOU ARE WILLING to step off the mound of your life and give the ball to the Master Coach.

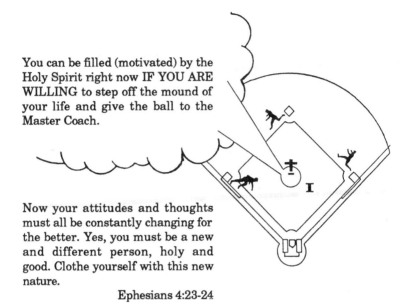

Now your attitudes and thoughts must all be constantly changing for the better. Yes, you must be a new and different person, holy and good. Clothe yourself with this new nature.
Ephesians 4:23-24

The Master Coach will not replace you on the mound against your heart's desire. Just as in receiving Christ, living consistently in His power is a matter of your will.

The Keys to Victory: Romans 6 (NAS)

A. KNOWING THIS, that our old self was crucified with Him that our body of sin might be done away with, that we should no longer be slaves to sin; for he who has died is freed from sin! (vs. 6-7)

B. Even so, CONSIDER YOURSELVES TO BE DEAD to sin, but alive to God in Christ Jesus. (v. 11)

C. But PRESENT YOURSELVES TO GOD as those alive from the dead, and your members as instruments of righteousness to God. (v. 13b)

PRESENT YOURSELF TO GOD THROUGH PRAYER

HERE IS A SUGGESTED PRAYER:

Dear Father,
I confess that I have taken control of my life and therefore have sinned against You. Thank You for forgiving me. I now CONSIDER myself dead to sin and PRESENT this body to You as a living sacrifice. I desire to be filled with Your Spirit as I live in obedience to Your WORD. Thank You for taking control of my life by the power of Your Spirit.
                                                      Amen.

HOW DO YOU KNOW YOU ARE FILLED BY THE HOLY SPIRIT?

And we are sure of this, that He WILL listen to us whenever we ask Him for ANYTHING IN LINE WITH HIS WILL. And if we really KNOW He is listening when we talk to Him and make our requests, then we CAN BE SURE that He will answer us.
                                                      I John 5:14-15

Is it God's will that you be filled (motivated) by His Spirit? He has said so (Ephesians 5:18). Therefore, based upon the authority of God's Word and His trustworthiness, you can KNOW you are filled with His Spirit regardless of your emotions.

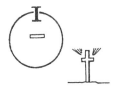

WHAT IF SELF TRIES TO GET BACK INTO THE GAME?

The self life is a deadly enemy of the control of the Holy Spirit. Often self will try to return to the game, and when that happens, Satan quickly reloads the bases. If you sense this happening, take these steps:

1) Confess all known sin to God and thank Him. He has forgiven you (I John 1:9).

2) Trust Christ to again fill you with the Holy Spirit, who will once more take control (Ephesians 5:18).

WHAT WILL GOD'S PERFECT RELIEVER ACCOMPLISH IN YOUR LIFE?

He will retire all doubt, fear, worry and other sins that run the bases of your life. He will substitute love, joy, peace and other fruits (Galatians 5:22-23). His assortment of pitches includes truth, faith, righteousness and other weapons through which daily victory is assured (Ephesians 6:10-18). He will turn your eyes to the Master Coach, Jesus Christ, and conform you to His likeness (II Corinthians 3:18). You can praise and thank God through trials and suffering in the game of life, knowing He has a plan for you (James 1:2-4). The final score will bring much glory to God!

For further information, please write:

WINNING RUN FOUNDATION
4539 Artelia Drive
Antioch, TN 37013

THE WINNING RUN FOUNDATION

THE WINNING RUN FOUNDATION is a non-profit organization established for the purpose of publishing athletic-related devotional materials. The WRF materials listed below are now available through the Fellowship of Christian Athletes, 8701 Leeds Road, Kansas City, MO 64129:

THE WINNING RUN
A 16-page booklet using baseball diagrams to explain salvation in Jesus Christ. (Also available in Spanish)

THE PERFECT SUBSTITUTE
A 16-page tract using the game of basketball to illustrate salvation in Jesus Christ. (Also available in French)

THE WINNING STROKE
A 16-page booklet using the game of golf to illustrate salvation in Jesus Christ.

THE PERFECT SAVE
A 16-page booklet using soccer illustrations to explain salvation in Jesus Christ. (Also available in Spanish, French, Russian and Polish)

TEMPLE CONDITIONING
A 4-page tract detailing the Biblical basis for physical fitness.

WISDOM FROM THE MASTER COACH
A 32-page devotional using athletic illustrations to highlight the book of Proverbs.

SERMON ON THE MOUND
A 32-page devotional study of Matthew 5-7 using baseball terms.

MORE THAN WINNERS
An 84-page devotional using Olympic illustrations in a study of Romans - Revelation.

GROWING STRONGER
A 20-page, fill-in-the-blank Bible Study, containing memory verses and diagrams designed to help rookies in the faith to comprehend the basics of Christian living
(Also available in Spanish)

HIGH HURDLES FOR GIRLS
A unique 64-page Devotional/Bible Study of sixteen "hurdles" faced by the female athlete as she "runs the great race of faith."

THE POINT AFTER
A 136-page paperback published by Zondervan (1987). This book uses athletic illustrations to highlight God's dealings in the lives of His people in both Old and New Testaments.

OUR GREAT AND AWESOME GOD
A 180-page paperback published by Wolgemuth and Hyatt (1990), using athletic illustrations to highlight the goodness, the greatness and the names of God.

OUR GREAT AND AWESOME SAVIOUR
Another Wolgemuth and Hyatt (1991) release using athletic illustrations to glorify the life and message of the Lord Jesus Christ. (210 pages)

STRONG IN SPIRITUAL WARFARE
A 184-page paperback using athletic illustrations in a study of Spiritual Warfare. A current and timely topic!

TRIUMPH IN TRIBULATION
A perfect-bound paperback on Psalms. This book, filled with athletic illustrations, presents Jesus Christ as our Rock, our Fortress, and our Deliverer in the most trying circumstances of life.